54 Reasons Why Parents Suck!

Dr Swati Lodha has been a mother, author, management guru and life coach for nearly two decades.

Swaraa Lodha is a 17-year-old student of Class XII. She is interested in music, photography and creative writing.

54 Reasons Why Parents Suck!
and Phew

★ Swati Lodha and Swaraa Lodha ★

RUPA

Published by
Rupa Publications India Pvt. Ltd 2018
7/16, Ansari Road, Daryaganj
New Delhi 110002

Sales centres:
Allahabad Bengaluru Chennai
Hyderabad Jaipur Kathmandu
Kolkata Mumbai

Copyright © Swati Lodha • Swaraa Lodha 2018

The views and opinions expressed in this book are the authors' own and the facts are as reported by them which have been verified to the extent possible, and the publishers are not in any way liable for the same.

All rights reserved.
No part of this publication may be reproduced, transmitted, or stored in a retrieval system, in any form or by any means, electronic, mechanical, photocopying, recording or otherwise, without the prior permission of the publisher.

ISBN: 978-93-5304-123-6

First impression 2018

10 9 8 7 6 5 4 3 2 1

The moral right of the authors has been asserted.

This book is sold subject to the condition that it shall not, by way of trade or otherwise, be lent, resold, hired out, or otherwise circulated, without the publisher's prior consent, in any form of binding or cover other than that in which it is published.

*To all the parents out there,
Whether it is to a cat, a company, a cause,
or sometimes even a child*

Contents

Why *Why Parents Suck* xi
Should a Mother Get Credit for Writing Such a Book? xvii

Reason 1:	Obedience Is the Password	1
Reason 2:	Sure, Your Child Is Amazing. But Have You Seen MINE?	6
Reason 3:	The 'P' Word	10
Reason 4:	Memory Is a Rumour	14
Reason 5:	Quirks Unlimited	18
Reason 6:	Where Is the Performance Appraisal?	22
Reason 7:	Delete 'What You Do', Download 'Who You Are'	26
Reason 8:	Tsunami of Social Media Messaging	30
Reason 9:	Awesome Wordsmiths, Awful Action-smiths	35
Reason 10:	We Attract Conflict, You Shun Conflict	39
Reason 11:	My Children Are Mine Only	45
Reason 12:	Claimers and Blamers	49
Reason 13:	Intention, Intention Go Away, Outcome Is Here to Stay	54
Reason 14:	Halo Effect	59
Reason 15:	I Act, Therefore I Am	63

Reason 16:	Paper or Plastic, or Both	67
Reason 17:	Opinion Overdose	72
Reason 18:	The P4: Permanent Persuasive Power of Parents	76
Reason 19:	Been There, Done That	81
Reason 20:	The Punishment Paradox	85
Reason 21:	Operate. Manipulate. Negotiate.	89
Reason 22:	Cryptic Cure of 'Cozy Consensus'	94
Reason 23:	More People, Less Responsibility	100
Reason 24:	Peaks and Ends	104
Reason 25:	The Perfect Child Syndrome	109
Reason 26:	You Resemble a Gorilla	114
Reason 27:	My Name is Spy...Digital Spy!	120
Reason 28:	Yesterday Ended Last Night	126
Reason 29:	Diamonds and Dirt	131
Reason 30:	The TINA Factor	136
Reason 31:	Observation Is a Dying Art. You Are the Living Example	141
Reason 32:	Who Moved My Creativity?	146
Reason 33:	Pervasive Parentisms	152
Reason 34:	Life in a 'Cell Phone'	158
Reason 35:	Hide and Deny	164
Reason 36:	We Live in Constant Summer	169
Reason 37:	I Love My Guilt	173
Reason 38:	You Are in a Relationship with Your Amygdala	177
Reason 39:	The 'What If' Buzzer	183
Reason 40:	Private Tutors, Surrogate Learning	188
Reason 41:	Rent a Car, Own a Ride	193
Reason 42:	Role-self Mash-up	197

Reason 43:	Blue and Pink	201
Reason 44:	Love Means Zero	209
Reason 45:	All Transmission and No Reception	214
Reason 46:	The 'C' and 'D' Words	218
Reason 47:	'Imbalance' Is the New 'Balance'	222
Reason 48:	Don't Change the Channel	227
Reason 49:	ATMs or Dads	231
Reason 50:	Quality Time Hogwash	236
Reason 51:	Why Did You Give Birth to Us?	240
Reason 52:	Have You Seen a Father Hero?	246
Reason 53:	Extreme Is the New Normal	251
Reason 54:	*Conditions Apply	254

Acknowledgements 259

Why *Why Parents Suck*

'Parents Suck' is a bold statement and I mean it.
My Economics teacher introduced me to the concept of VUCA: Volatility, Uncertainty, Complexity and Ambiguity.

I nodded, not because I understood the macro world in these terms but because I saw my micro world there—my VUCA parents.

When I was an infant, they were Volatile, as most of the time they didn't know what to do with the tiny piece of mayhem that would poop, cry, sleep and fall sick without sending any notifications.

As I grew up, they became more Uncertain of my growth trajectory as well as their competence in nurturing me. Constant comparison with other parents would make them further uncertain.

In my tweens, our relationship turned into a see-saw, turning them into crazy balls of Complexity. One minute, they would punish me and please me in the next. One minute, they would guide me and grumble in the next.

My adolescence has hit them harder, our relationship hinges on Ambiguity. It is a snake and ladder game of horror and hope.

The title of this book pops up in the head of every Indian child in those daily moments of exasperation when we wish parents came with a mute button.

Don't get me wrong. I love these two individuals whom I call my parents. I am just overwhelmed by their obsession—me. They fuss over me, they go to incredible heights, unbelievable depths and unsurmountable widths to make me the best child they can ever have.

A man in his late sixties suspects that his wife is going deaf, so he decides to test her hearing. He stands at the opposite end of the living room from her and asks, 'Can you hear me?'

No answer.

He moves halfway across the room towards her and asks again, 'Can you hear me?'

Still no answer.

He moves further and comes to stand right beside her and asks, 'Can you hear me now?'

'For the third time, yes!' she replies.

The problem lies in us but we are hell-bent on believing that it lies in others. Our parents fit this description completely.

In the USA, after heart disease and cancer, medical care ranks as the nation's third biggest killer. Drugs, which are designed to cure diseases kill 1,00,000 people every year and the number doesn't include accidental overdoses.[1]

Thousands of patients are operated upon unnecessarily and many get infected. Many doctors, who are obviously expected to cure patients, become the reason of their poor health resulting in death.

Similarly, many parents who are obviously expected to love, encourage, nurture and guide their children, become the reason behind their low self-esteem, emotional turbulence and helplessness, leading to irreparable damage and sometimes death.

I recently stumbled upon a statistical gem in a newspaper

---

[1]https://hub.jhu.edu/2016/05/03/medical-errors-third-leading-cause-of-death/

which reported that over a period of fourteen years, 20,000 people died in various terror attacks in India; however, there were 38,585 murders and 79,189 suicides for love related reasons in the same period. Not only this, 39,775 students killed themselves between 2005 and 2015. It means that our emotional disturbances, our socio-culturescape are causing six times more deaths than terrorists.[2]

We love to talk about terrorism as a major problem because it is dramatic and distant. Our emotional and psychological turbulence does not jolt us out of our inertia because it is as common as cough and cold. People keep killing their lovers, jilted ones keep committing suicides and students keep hanging their boots. It is so mainstream!

Should we not be addressing our social malice with an acute urgency? We are extremely worried about the relationship status of India and China while the relationships within the family do not bother us. Growing up today is an art which needs strategic tools to survive and loads of love to blossom. I wish I could initiate a perceptual change in parents through this book which could enhance communication in families, reduce conflicts and forge a value-centric culture.

My mother ardently admires the investor-authors Charlie Munger and Warren Buffett for their life philosophy. Charlie Munger, known for his inverted thought process, says that to understand how businesses become strong, he studies how businesses fail; to understand how to be happy in life, he studies how to make life miserable.[3] To seek good judgement, collect

---

[2] http://www.deccanchronicle.com/lifestyle/viral-and-trending/040417/more-indians-die-because-of-love-than-terror-attacks.html
[3] Foreword to the authorized Chinese translation of Peter D. Kaufman's

instances of bad judgement, is his belief.

I agree with the wisdom tank of this old man who asserts that very smart people do very dumb things.

Many of these smart people are the smart parents. Their smartness is eaten up by their dumbness when they show their ego, greed, envy, fear and mindless imitation of others.[4]

Parents show mammoth egos in front of their children. They are greedy to have nothing but the best for them. They envy other parents and children who perform better than theirs. They are fearful forever. They believe in collective wisdom of the crowd. All these parental actions cause serious problems for us. And that is why we have attempted to compile fifty-four of such follies which should be corrected.

54 Reasons Why Parents Suck talks about the various beliefs, behaviours and biases held by most Indian parents that make them annoying and difficult. These fifty-four chapters are fifty-four signposts that tell us what parents do wrong, why they do it and how not to do so.

Though parents never like to believe that they can go wrong, the truth is we all go wrong. It could be unintentional, habitual or out of ignorance but it is harming the lives of almost all the children.

No parent would agree with all the fifty-four reasons but each parent would surely agree with some, if they begin with honest acceptance and a willingness to improve their

---

Poor Charlie's Almanack: The Wit and Wisdom of Charles T. Munger (*2010*, PCA Publications).
[4]Warren Buffet on Adam Smith's *Money Game*, Transcript No. 105, aired on 15 May 1998.

relationship with their children.

The signs of great parenting are reflected in a parent's behaviour, and not the child's. If you guys falter, we will surely do the same.[5]

Let us try and raise our games together.

—Swaraa

---

[5] www.trueparenting.net

Should a Mother Get Credit for Writing Such a Book?

Am I Lord Ganesha who was handpicked by Ved Vyasa to write his Mahabharata?

When the journey of the book began, I was.

I am one of those lifelong learners of leadership and excellence—whom some people call experts.

Through my recent book, *Don't Raise Your Children, Raise Yourself*, I pulled Parenting into the arena of leadership—sacred and soulful leadership, as I put it.

Swaraa accompanied me during one of the many promotional events for the book. The moderator of the talk asked her in jest, 'Your mom helps other parents become better. How do you like your Mom? Is she perfect?'

'I like her. But nobody is perfect.'

'Tell us one thing that you don't like in her as a parent.'

'Oh! I could write a book!' she quipped.

And that's how it started.

Since she said it spontaneously, I knew it was true.

And since she was in Class XI, she said she didn't have the time to write a book.

So, I offered to become Lord Ganesha to her.

But soon, I became what Hermione Granger was to Harry Potter—a logical adviser, a guide in crisis and a dependable worker.

Swaraa would say her thoughts aloud and move on, leaving me to nibble of the apple of reasons why I sucked—why so many of us did.

Since the seeds of many reasons germinated in the mind of a 16-year-old, I have written the book in the voice of a 16-year-old.

Together, we had daily half-hour sessions for two months to bounce off different reasons. We listed eighty-three of them, finally bringing them down to fifty-four. She made a questionnaire and sent it to her schoolmates, friends, family friends and friends of friends and received feedback from around 186 children of ages between 8 and 16. It was totally confidential, as we didn't know who responded out of the five hundred children contacted. And who wrote what.

After I finished the manuscript, I mailed it to her.

'Give me two weeks. Thanks,' she sent back a reply.

Three weeks and two reminders later, she sent the manuscript with a witty makeover. So, whenever you break into a smile while reading, bless Swaraa for that.

The whole process of coming up with this unconventional idea—thinking, brooding, arguing, sulking and writing—was an incredible tale of adventure and anguish. We, as a mother-daughter team, explored our own relationship amidst claims and blames, tears and sarcasm.

It was therapeutic and transformational, because we kept our egos aside and decided to be radically transparent. We hope it enables you to do the same.

Wait a minute.

If you guys think that I am neither Lord Ganesha nor Hermione Granger, am I Vibhishana, then?

After all, I have shaken hands with the tribe of children against the tribe of parents.

Well, I am fine with being Vibhishana, too, as long as it helps you to reach out to your children in a more meaningful way and enables you to walk on a bridge of love and empathy together, hand in hand.

—Swati Lodha,
A mother and an enabler

REASON 1

Obedience Is the Password

I am indirectly disobeying my father by writing this book. He would never want me to do this. But still, here goes.

I have a major obedience issue with my father whenever we travel. I like to carry my laptop and camera with me, instead of packing them in the luggage. Every time we are at the airport, as is the norm, I have to take these out of my hand baggage during the security check, which takes some time. My father, therefore, insists that I should pack my laptop in the check-in baggage. Thus, each time we travel, he tells me to pack the laptop, and, each time, I refuse to do so.

'For you, things are more important than people,' was his exasperated statement during our last travel.

Dear parents, you want us to obey because you think that you are always right. You firmly believe that all our actions should branch out from the root of obedience.

If I don't obey you, you staunchly believe that:

- I am ignorant. I don't know what you want me to know.
- I am dumb. I lack the competence to understand what you want me to understand.
- I am a devil. I simply want to defy you.

Am I ignorant if I care about damaging or losing an expensive gadget?

Am I dumb if I am ready to carry the heavy load because I value my laptop which you paid for with your hard-earned money?

Am I a devil who wants to annoy her own Dad during each air travel?

In my responsible behaviour, my father sees defiance.

Why do you trust your thoughts and opinions so much?

'We have seen the world', is your universal answer to all our arguments.

Have you seen Taiwan? Guatemala?

Nobody can see the whole world unless you are an Indian God.

There are three possibilities pertaining to obedience.

- We obey you readily because we agree with you and believe that you are right.
- My research questionnaire[1] suggests that most of us obey our parents when we are unsure of ourselves. Obeying you becomes our automated behaviour. It makes things easier as we get someone to blame for our actions—all the time. Most Indian marriages must be a result of automated obedience!
- We obey you to maintain sanity. I obey you to avoid the mess that disagreement would generate. When I do so for issues trivial to me, it hurts less. However, when I have to agree to your diktat for issues that are important to me, it is an unforgivable damage. This obedience is out of fear in the beginning—we fear your authority—and gradually, some of us start challenging it while some shut themselves into a shell. Does the increasing number of suicides among teenagers ring

---

[1]https://docs.google.com/forms/d/e/1FAIpQLSeTwb3t5wlNrr3RdQ5uVObW6b7ykIvEBWip_ixh3UituZLzjw/viewform

a bell? I cannot forget a letter that a girl wrote to her mother before taking her life. The mother aspired to make her an engineer while she wanted to write, and her beautifully crafted long letter showed a glimpse of the writer she could have been.[2]

- We obey you in anticipation of reward. Many of you wriggle out the desired obedience through transactions. Some of us will always do it and some of us might give it up after getting tired of the puppetry. Whenever we disagree with you, irrespective of how big or small the matter is, how young or old we are, how cool or critical the situation is, you get hurt.

You love your authority as parents far more than you love us as people. You should. You must. But, in a reasonable way, and that, too, if your child is someone who messes up and doesn't own up to his or her mistake. If s/he repeats the same mistakes, if s/he copies you by saying 'no' (to everything!), if it is a real life-threatening situation, only then can you show your authority and that, too, to help us—and not to feel good for being the superior one. For normal growing-up glitches like keeping a room messy (according to your cleaning standards that you set after growing up), forgetting to switch the alarm on, not enjoying your jokes and your parties, not getting grades to your satisfaction, arguing with you, should you behave like a non-stop whining daily TV soap?

Business executive, author and philanthropist, Vineet

---

[2] http://www.indiatimes.com/news/world/suicide-note-of-iit-aspirant-made-public-kriti-tripathi-wanted-to-be-an-astronaut-not-engineer-994680-294060.html

Nayar, recently shared that he had great respect for this generation's intellect, which has a different attitude towards authority and direction.[3]

Thank you, Mr Nayar, for understanding me and my whole generation. We want to work with you, not for you. Before my parents order me to stop reading such stuff, I will jump on to this research study:

Stanley Milgram, a famous American psychologist conducted an electric shock study to examine how much pain and suffering ordinary people could inflict on others when they were told by someone to do it. Around 60 per cent of them continued to administer lethal shocks to participants because they were told by a man in a white coat to do so.[4] Such admiration for authority!

You expect us to behave like those people who were administering electric shocks without giving any thought to the well-being of the anxious participants. We do it too—by hurting our own well-being.

We stay loyal to you by staying loyal to your beliefs. We love you and hence stick to all that you teach. We win your attachment but we lose our individuality. We hold on to your opinions, your lessons because we want to hold on to you. If we try to discard some of your ideas, we feel that you will feel that we are diminishing our relationship.

Have you ever wondered that you feel safer when you drive a car than when you fly in a plane? The reason is simple. You feel more in control when you are behind the wheel, than when someone else is flying the plane. But your feeling cannot

---

[3] https://hbr.org/2010/05/do-we-get-gen-why.html
[4] https://www.simplypsychology.org/milgram.html

change the fact that road accidents are far more rampant and life-threatening than flight accidents. Your belief that by being a controlling parent, you will save us from future accidents, is naïve.

Why is obedience and loyalty overrated in a parent–child relationship? How about learning to re-calibrate your illusion of control as we move forward?

You consider disagreement as disrespect and a child disrespecting the holy parent is the ultimate sin.

Disagreement is NOT disrespect. Can you guys get that?

If controlling is your raising mechanism, defying is our learning mechanism.

REASON 2

Sure, Your Child Is Amazing. But Have You Seen MINE?

When my mother's friend was looking for a house to buy, she shortlisted three places—A, B and C.

Option C was the least preferred because the view from the flat was not scenic and the building was older. They liked B as the view was amazing but it was priced higher. They were about to finalize A, but the seller backed out at the eleventh hour and they had to finally settle for C.

Suddenly, C became the best buy in all their conversations. So many advantages popped out from every corner of the house that flat C became their most valued proposition. The view became 'vibrant', which was 'concrete' earlier. The building which was 'old and used' became 'better constructed as better material was used a decade ago than now'.

If we are selling something, we charge more for it than what we ourselves would be willing to spend. Parents also fall prey to the 'Endowment Effect' because they are emotionally attached to their children. They add more value and importance to the competencies of their children like the seller adds more zeroes to the price of the product he owns.

Every baker feels that his flour comes from the best farm and his dough is the most consistent and light, because he is attached to his own produce. Parents suffer from 'Motivated Blindness'[5]

---

[5]Max H. Bezerman and Ann E. Tenbrunsel. 2011. *Blind Spots: Why We*

towards their children. They find them more hard-working and more talented than the rest out of their love for them.

Each landlord feels that he is renting out the best maintained property with the sturdiest furniture and the most beautiful curtains because he has invested his time in buying the stuff. Each parent feels the same towards their children because they have a sense of ownership and emotional investment. It has nothing to do with 'who we are' but everything to do with 'who you are to us'.

We become more valued by the sheer virtue of belonging to you.

Any award that we win becomes more prestigious than others, any bike that you buy for us is the best possible product—even my new class teacher becomes more proficient than the older one.

If you find me and some other person vying for a particular thing, you would want me to have it anyhow. You would try to make it accessible for me because you can't see someone else gain it. Someone else gaining it will hurt you more than me losing it.

My loss becomes your personal loss. My failure is more personal to you than it is to me. It becomes more painful when someone else (it is worse if you know them) succeeds at it.

To hide that personalized pain, you would go an extra mile to find some anomaly in that thing or the person who succeeds.

If I play chess, brain power is certainly more valuable than physical exercise.

If I am a wrestler, it is the most strategic sport.

Fail to Do What's Right and What to Do About it. Princeton, NJ: Princeton University Press. p. 81.

Not only this, you guys begin appreciating us with the opening line, 'I am not saying it because he is my son, he is genuinely...'

We seem brighter and bigger to you. We are like a Snapchat story to which you gleefully add different filters and colour schemes, and share enthusiastically with the world.

Many of you overvalue us more in front of family and your friends. You do so to magnify your own stature and social standing. You would judge us objectively in private but create an amplified aura in public. Everyone loves trophies that can make good Facebook (FB) posts and cute profile pictures. It improves your digital stature cascading into a better social standing. It establishes you as an efficient parent. You feel 'on top of the world' because others are seething inside while smiling on the outside.

In front of others, you would even exaggerate our performance.

'My son got 91 per cent marks in Class X.'

'Is this the aggregate?' asks a friend.

'Yes.'

The reality is a little less appealing. Actually, it is the average of the top five scores out of eight subjects which the school considers for granting scholarship. For you, it is almost the same because he is YOUR son.

How about trying to be honest? After all, if you guys don't deal with reality, reality will eventually deal with you.

Parents are masters of showcasing what they or their children have achieved. They do not mind changing the original targets to suit their competence. As Rolf Dobelli in his book, *The Art of Thinking Clearly*, says, 'It is the equivalent of shooting an arrow and drawing a bull's eye around where it lands.'[6]

'My son got admitted to Patiala College of Engineering.'

'Patiala College of Engineering! Oh!' the friend says sympathetically.

'That was his first choice. He liked that college the best.'

'Yeah, sure!'

Parents tend to be overconfident in their estimates of our future as they do not factor in uncertainties. A 'pre-mortem' will help wherein parents imagine a future failure and try to find its cause. It will reduce optimism and help parents prepare a backup plan.

Parents wish to spin complete narratives of success for us even when failure is always embedded in it. This overvaluation is scary and unrealistic. It gives us false hopes and unrealistic sense of self. I start to feel like Virat Kohli as soon as I pick the cricket bat.

How about taking an outside view—finding out real-life failure stories of those who treaded similar paths? How about equipping us with survival tools for future rather than Photoshopping our present selves?

---

[6]Rolf Dobelli. 2013. *The Art of Thinking Clearly.* New York: HarperCollins.

REASON 3

The 'P' Word

The word 'Parent' has so much importance, respect and responsibility attached to it that couples become very serious after getting the tag of 'Parents'. Get two aliens who do not know the word 'Parent' and give them a newborn. They will do a much better job than these parents who are under pressure to perform as 'Parents'.

A friend of my Dad is called 'Sharma ji' by everyone. One day, he called on the home phone and when I asked who was speaking, he replied, 'Sharma ji speaking.'

We begin to see ourselves the way others 'see' us. A parent, especially a mother, is expected to 'be all' for her child and hence she tries to become an acutely aspirational mom who keeps benchmarking herself against the fleet of moms sailing in the same boat.

A new mother starts treating her husband like an infant.

'Did you eat your lunch properly?'

'Of course you will feel tired, if you don't sleep on time.'

Ugh!

A new father associates every problem with the problems caused by a newborn.

'You are just like my newborn. Always tired.'

'You are just like my baby. No worries in the world because we are there to clean up after you.'

Ugh!

As 'new' parents, the 'P' word shapes your world view. You

tend to ardently believe that how we turn out will depend solely on your actions as parents. Alas, this is as 'wrong' as 'wrong' can get. We are a crazy mix of your genes, family behaviours, socio-economic levels, schooling, discrimination, luck, illness and many such factors. More so, we all are dynamic people who change faster than the flight of a cheetah.

Can you attribute population explosion in our country to one cause? Can you blame one reason for the Indo–Pak conflict? Even if you blame it on one reason, there would be many others supporting reasons, big and small.

You cannot be the only people who can be credited or blamed for how your children turn out. Judith Rich Harris, in her book, *The Nurture Assumption*, states that the influence of parents on children is diluted by the effect of peer pressure as they grow up.[7]

Had it all been because of parents, how is it that the brother of a talented scientist turned out to be a kidnapper? How is it that the son of a reputed, rich lawyer couple landed up in jail? How is it that the daughter of a single, uneducated mother cracked the civil service exam?

Most parents give too much importance to their own actions, falsely believing that each action—from reading a story daily to attending a weekly music class—contributes heavily to the shining future of their children. Our personalities are not direct results of your persistent priming towards perfection.

Had life been similar to mathematics, linear answers would have been possible. Please distance yourself from us a bit so that our picture can be clearer to you.

---

[7]Judith R. Harris. 1998. *The Nurture Assumption: Why Children Turn Out the Way They Do.* New York: Free Press.

When a person gets the identity of a 'Hostel Warden', s/he behaves like a 'strict disciplinarian, punctual and fastidious' person. Whereas, when a person gets the identity of a team worker, he behaves in a 'collaborative, self-sacrificing' way.[8] Similarly, as soon as an individual gets the identity of a 'parent', s/he starts behaving in a 'controlling, nagging, overly-involved' manner. Why are you so hard on yourself as a parent? You are too much in self-criticism mode and then you try to pass it over to us.

You wanted a specific career and you got into something else.

You expected a promotion and someone else got it.

You dreamt of an intelligent, beautiful baby and then you got me.

You are tough on yourself which makes you focus disproportionately on your negative attributes.

It has, in turn, two negative impacts on us: Firstly, we also pick, 'being hard on ourselves' as a survival tool. We start to believe that it is good to demoralize oneself. Secondly, we get judged harshly by you. You are hard on us, because life according to you has been hard on you. You don't count your blessings and don't let us count ours. You instil fear in us to count our burdens.

Why can't you be off the leash? Why can't you love yourselves the way we love you? Be kinder to yourselves. We can cheer

---

[8]If you change someone's identity you can also change his or her behaviour, says 'Tiny Habits' guru B.J. Fogg. (http://www.behaviormodel.org/)

ourselves by being our own cheerleaders.

When I make a mistake, you say, 'I think I am failing as a mother.' When I don't understand something, you say, 'What did I do wrong that this is happening to me?' (I am sorry, but I think Indian soaps would benefit from your brilliance and eloquence when writing dialogues, rather than me!)

If it helps you, should I stop addressing you as 'Mom' or 'Dad'? I tried that, and it seemed to work till I was about seven or eight. After that, it had no impact for a while and then it became worse.

I have always called my dad 'Bubzie'—my version of his name. For a few years, he was actually a friend, a peer who was my coolest team member. I would address him without any pretence and stereotypical inhibitions and he responded while disguising himself as a 'cool dude.' But his 'father' identity hit him hard in the forthcoming years, cascading into every corner of my life. When I dress up, his 'fatherness' pops into my thinking bubble, judging the length of my dress. When I go for a school dance, his X-ray eyes will try to judge my date in the twenty seconds of 'dropping me off.' When I want to watch a movie, his secret reviewers will tell him exactly where the romance occurs and exactly at that moment, he will start discussing my future with me right in the middle of the theatre!

This is what the 'P' word does to you. How about taking the monkey off your back?

REASON 4

Memory Is a Rumour

I have an uncle—let's call him 'X'—whose childhood is a story I prefer way over well-written novels. Whenever they get together, my mom and her cousins inevitably come to, 'Do you remember what X had done to Y at Z time of the day?'

Through their throwback gossip sessions, I found out that, on one occasion, my uncle covered his father's brand-new car with mud. I am fortunate to have seen a picture of that 11-year-old, rebellious boy smirking next to the muddy Fiat.

On another occasion, the very same uncle smashed the TV screen with a stool. Once, he slept for twenty hours straight because he wanted to miss his CA exam. Out of curiosity, I asked him if he had shared his adventures with his kids. He refused and said, 'No way'. He added that he had told them about his bad temper so that they don't misbehave much.

Wow, how convenient!

It is always good to remember oneself as an exemplary individual, in hindsight.

All of you were such ideal children who had tough parents, tougher times, but you all survived, thanks to your grit, discipline and obedience.

At least, this is what you want your children to believe.

You guys use your memory as a strategic tool to keep us on a leash. 'When we were young...' erupts out of your memory-filled mouth every time you disapprove of something—which is as frequent as the breakdown of my Wi-Fi connectivity.

You forget that memory is transient. Accuracy disappears from it over time, but you stick to your version of the fact which you had absentmindedly registered in the first place, and is long forgotten now.

When you meet an old friend or a cousin and they remind you of some incidents from your childhood, your brain adds detailed false memories to it based on their additional information. Every negative or positive memory of childhood turns into a memory projecting you in a positive light.

Were you all so perfect or are your brains so smart to turn memories into incidents filled with inaccuracies.

Your childhood's stories are never factual. They are filled with 'Flashbulb memories'[9], which are flawed and products of reconstruction.

Whatever you did as children, how you felt as children—you have subconsciously adjusted your past to fix the present so that you can easily hide your mistakes and make us, your own children, look like embodiments of wrongdoing.

What happened to you were facts, what you remember are autobiographical stories which are easy to change, interesting to narrate and have an appreciating value with time. Each fact turns into a story—a happy, sad, emotional, or scary one—which is something that is far from facts.

I have never been on school trips because my parents are never comfortable sending me out alone. Our school took us to Singapore two years ago. My dad said, 'Oh! We have been

---

[9] Flashbulb memories are recollections that a person may have of the circumstances associated with a dramatic event. Though these memories are highly vivid, there are significant inconsistencies in most people's memories.

there before.' Travelling with my parents and travelling with school friends is as similar as Kumar Sanu and Shakira.

And last year, when our school trip was to Indonesia, my mother said, 'We will go there next year.' I wanted to go as that would have been my last trip with school friends, but I accepted that they were not interested in sending me.

Suddenly, on the last day of name submission, my father said, 'Go, if you want to.'

'It is too late. I don't want to go now,' I said.

'Fine. Don't tell me later that I did not allow you.'

Wow!

I am pretty sure how memories of my school trips are going to be stored in their minds for future.

In ten years' time, my parents would refer to this chunk of memory as: 'When you were very young, we were not sure that you would be able to take care of yourself without us. So, we did not send you to school trips. When you got older, we allowed you but you did not want to go.'

In hindsight, the reality will get a twist.

All parents suffer from 'Hindsight Bias'[10] because all the bumpy roads of their childhood and ours become as smooth as racing tracks in the present. They seem to prove it to us that their lives have completely turned out to be the way they had predicted and planned. They seem to believe that their present success is a clear-cut result of all the hard work and efforts during school and college years. You convincingly tell us, 'I always wanted to work for an MNC' or 'I worked towards

---

[10] Hindsight bias is when, after an event occurs, we feel we already knew what was going to happen. Hindsight bias is also sometimes called the I-knew-it-all-along phenomenon.

my dream of becoming a doctor', when the reality could be strikingly different.

You remember your past in accordance with your present feelings and opinions, which are certainly distinct from feelings and opinions of your younger self.

We get a truer, clearer picture if our grandparents remember the heartburns you gave them and if they are ready to share your true childhood with us. Everyone makes mistakes and everyone remembers the mistakes committed by others. How about sharing the real slices of your lives with us along with the life stories of other friends and family?

REASON 5

Quirks Unlimited

All moms know Linda Goodman for sure. There is a chance that they might not know who Sarvepalli Radhakrishnan was. As soon as they meet another mom or a girl, they want to know her zodiac sign and their camaraderie hits a new high if they share sun signs.

I am not sure whether I am a carefree, straightforward person because I am often told that these are the traits of my zodiac sign or my zodiac sign is the cause of these traits in me.

British researcher Geoffrey Dean calls people born at the same moment in the same place as 'time twins'. If planetary positions predict personalities of people, such people should be leading pretty similar lives but Dean found no such similarity despite conducting extensive research for many years on thousands of 'time twins'.

Your belief influences our behaviour as you keep reiterating the traits of our zodiac signs and we align ourselves using the golden rule: MOM IS ALWAYS RIGHT.

Not only this, you guys have at least one 'Guru' in your life whom you worship, apart from the numerous images and idols of different Gods that I bow my head to. Your unflinching faith is based on some miraculous incidents and hearsay which we need to believe in.

You guys manipulate spellings of every family member's name when numerologists, made famous by some celebrity, offer consultation to you.

Some of you have even altered our birth dates so that we could save a valuable year of kindergarten studies. (If a child completes six years of age between September and December, he doesn't get admission in July and has to wait for a year.)

So you play with the date.

I wish you planned better rather than leaving us with two birthdays to remember and use.

Some foresighted parents even plan the births to make them auspicious.

Doctored birthdays and engineered spellings with imposed personality traits—all for our good.

Well, you can't blame me for my actions. Blame my zodiac sign and the numerologist. Consult the cosmos while I sing 'Fault in the Stars'.

Many surveys in the USA and Britain reveal that about 75 to 80 per cent of the people are a little superstitious.

Without any such research in India, I can vouch for more than 90 per cent Indians believing in many superstitions. As we see our parents performing so many rituals, we end up doing the same—I will chant 101 times if I pass Maths, I will go to this temple if my crush sees my message.

As I see you taking refuge in pearl rings, evil eye bracelets, sacrificial yagnas, it impacts me hard. My grandmother would consult the Hindu almanac (choghadiya) before even buying a pair of shoes. She wouldn't allow us to leave the house unless a two-wheeler crossed our path. Now I wait for the same and inadvertently get late. Your superstitions silence my rationality just the way your glaring eyes silence my mouth.

Parents fear problems and love everyone and everything that claims to solve their problems. Since we are the most valuable assets they have, most of their problems revolve around us.

'Babaji, my child is 5 and still does not speak much.'

'Guruji, my child keeps his room locked and does not listen to me.'

'Swamiji, bless him so that he makes it to IIT.'

To smoothen our paths and stay relevant in our lives, they hang on to all such godmen who offer relief to their 'anxious for no reason' souls.

Apart from giving your superstitions to us, you give us a name too. I am sure you know that we will carry our names with us for all our lives.

I am amazed by those parents who have helped us have four 'Vedants' and three 'Khushis' in our class of eighty kids.

I understand that each year has a popularity chart for names. You must have picked either the most trending name (Aarav in 2006 or Amayra in 2016) or the name of a person you loved. (I might neither love the person nor the name.)

If parents are so whimsical to name us 'Zoi Pandharpur' or 'Svetlana Sandookwala', we should be given a chance to edit our names without their interference and emotional outbursts.

I wish they could give three options in the birth certificate and we could at least choose any one of them later. A lot of experts would have surely helped them to find three different names reflecting three different personalities. We would have picked the one that suits us best.

Can you beat the weirdness of those parents who, even after Hurricane Katrina created havoc in Mississippi and Louisiana in 2005, continue to name their daughters Katrina, and that too, in the same places?

Is this the only name you want your daughter to have to be a reminder of massive destruction?

A victim of parents' quirkiness shared that his mother did not let him buy a motorbike by his favourite brand—Yamaha—because she was uncomfortable by the word 'Yama' in it.

Another quirk-survivor shared that he wanted to buy a cycle which was marketed as 'Devil' by Hero Cycles. His mom allowed him to buy the same only when he agreed to strike the 'L' at the end of 'Devil' and change it to 'Devi'.

These automobile companies cannot understand our plight. They have no clue about the number of obstacles we need to cross to finally make it to that bike or motorbike.

How about offering a choice between 'Vikramaditya', 'Vivaan' or 'Vin' or a 'Sanghmitra', 'Shanaya' and 'Sheryl'?

Your fear and will to control makes superstitions the 'low hanging fruit'. Superstitions act like alternate therapies for problem solving. A parent without fear is a rare gem. How about bracing yourself to go through these trials of life that sets an exemplary path for us too?

REASON 6

Where Is the Performance Appraisal?

We are judged, evaluated and labelled as 'good boy', 'naughty girl', 'topper', 'selfish', 'very fair', 'little heavy', 'bad at English', 'sucks at dance'. We get punished in real time.

A tantrum thrown.
A slap received.
A word mispronounced.
A demeaning laughter echoed.

You have various methods up your sleeve to set us right. Mothers shout and sob, fathers stare and shut their mouths. Then they reverse their actions sometimes. And when they do, we know all hell has broken loose. Every day, our performance is under the scanner at school, sports clubs, activity classes and home.

Your performance is judged, assessed and appraised at your workplace but nobody ever reviews your competence as a family person. And we cannot even try to review it, because *how would a 16-year-old know anything about his own parents?*

We know how formal ACRs (Annual Confidentiality Reports) and 'Performance Measurement' systems smack of supremacy and secrecy leaving not enough room for two-way communication and constructive feedback. The way you feel dissatisfied and short-changed after getting reviewed through these lifeless methods is exactly how we feel in the absence of real communication.

As a toddler, I can't reach to your level but you surely can bend down. Since it requires time and energy with serious mindful intent to understand me, bending down doesn't happen very often.

You look down, literally and figuratively.

As a tween, I start arguing and crave for a dialogue but it turns into a debate.

Since you like 'either/or' instead of 'and', you give us the 'listening' part of the deal while keeping the 'talking' part to yourself.

You tell us that test scores, weekly assessments and parental guidance will help us to play to our potential. We also want to tell you that our daily conversations (where we talk and you listen without any digital diversion), weekly discussions (without any crashing china or teary tantrums) and yearly reflections (where mistakes are honestly accepted) would help you prune your parentability.

We propose to execute our CDR (Converse, Discuss, Reflect) plan with you where you remember that 'Parent' is a role. A role is about what people expect from you. It should not be confused with your 'Self'. What we expect from your 'Parent' role is of importance. When we get agitated with the boundaries you set, we are showing our dissatisfaction with your parental role. We should be allowed to air our expectations from you at different stages of our journey. Though we hear about 'unconditional love' of parents, it becomes a myth due to its obvious absence. Unconditional love and support is our constant unmet expectation.

We might set up some norms of actions and behaviours which are jointly owned by us. An informal performance measurement and a review (may be orchestrated by grandparents) won't hurt.

Our feedback will certainly help you become a parent we will be proud of.

We are not proud of those parents who play 'cool', who play to the gallery, who become 'YES' parents. Agreeing to our 'unreasonable' demands, giving in to our tantrums is not about earning brownie points for a performance review.

We expect to create an environment where a two-way communication is possible, listening happens and disagreement is welcome.

A great example is the film production company Pixar, which is an incredible content creator in the uncertain world of film-making with several blockbusters to its credit. The secret lies in the creative process deeply embedded in the members of Pixar Braintrust—a group of Pixar colleagues which meets every few months to openly review the progress of a film in development. 'The license to criticise (more like shooting holes in each other's ideas), combined with the ability to take criticism, became a strong bond between the members of the Braintrust.'[11]

Can we create such a soul-searching process which will certainly be difficult to create and brutal to execute, but the benefits, in the form of a lifelong connect between us, will outweigh the mental and emotional roadblocks we might hit?

---

[11]Christopher Finch says so in his 2013 book, *The CG Story: Computer-Generated Animation and Special Effects* (The Monacelli Press).

A vulnerable and volatile family is far more connected and bonded than a picture-perfect and pleasant one. A stand-up comedian gets a feedback every 15 seconds, children get it in 5 seconds. Parents should at least get it sometimes.

On Airbnb, there is a mutual 'rate and review' system followed by the travellers who stay in homes and the owners who rent them out. The travellers rate the facilities and comfort provided by the homeowner but the homeowner reserves the right to rate the behaviour and resource handling of the traveller. Why not be fair in your parental role too?

I recently read a question on Quora[12]: 'Can a child of helicopter parents sue them for harassment after s/he turned 18?'

Though punishment seems far-fetched and purposeless, an honest appraisal will help all of us. A lot of people are good at pleasing their bosses and hence it is believed that while selecting such people for jobs, references should be taken not from their bosses/superiors but from peers and subordinates. Similarly, we are the best to appraise our parents.

---

[12]Quora is a popular online platform to share knowledge and experience by asking questions, getting answers and connecting with people with unique insights and quality answers.

REASON 7

Delete 'What You Do', Download 'Who You Are'

I read *Freakonomics*[13] two years ago in Class X. The authors' views about being a perfect parent compelled me to think about the modus operandi of Indian parents.

There is not much data from the Indian horizon to prove it, but I will surely tell you about the Early Childhood Longitudinal Study (ECLS), regularly undertaken by the US Department of Education.[14]

This rich study covered twenty thousand children around one thousand US schools over two decades to find answers to questions like:

- Which activities of parents improve performance of children?
- Which factors, like income of parents, age of mother at the time of childbirth, education level of parents influence the academic/social performance of a child?

For us to understand why our parents suck, let me focus on three findings of one such study discussed by economists Steven D. Levitt and Stephen J. Dubner in their book.

---

[13]Steven D. Levitt and Stephen J. Dubner. 2011. *Freakonomics: A Rogue Economist Explores the Hidden Side of Everything*. New York: William Morrow.
[14]Ibid. pp. 147–62.

First, it matters for a child's future if he had low birth weight but it doesn't matter if he joined a talent development programme.

Having low birth weight means the child belongs to parents who have less resources, or a mother who smokes or drinks or had a stressful pregnancy. Low birth weight hurts the future prospects of a child, but joining a federal programme like Head Start doesn't give any boost to his performance. It means that parents need to work upon their health—mental and physical—rather than working on their children by putting them into fancy preschool programmes.

A stressed mom will do me more harm than any good done by attending various grooming classes at a young age. My mom, being an amazing artist herself (all the walls of my home bear testimony to it), religiously sent me to drawing classes for three consecutive years. I was as persistent at not learning as my mom was in sending me to those classes. She kept buying sheets and pencils and I kept drawing wobbly stick figures. Rather than trying to make me a junior Hussain, she should have honed her sketching skills.

The second finding states that it matters for a child's future if parents speak English at home but it doesn't matter if they regularly take them to the museums.

Having English-speaking parents mean they can help their children prepare better for tests. They can improve their abilities to understand and communicate. But going to museums to understand history and culture doesn't impact the test scores of a child.

I can totally understand the authors' finding. I have disliked all the museums that my parents have insisted me to see. The only thing I remember after each visit is a deep urge to snuggle in my bed and sleep. When I was three, they took me to Disneyland in Hong Kong. I have no memory of that trip, the same way I have no memory of my recent exams. The domestic folklore has it that my dad lost his camera at Disneyland and hence there are no clicked memories either. Well, before you think that I am digressing from my argument, let me clarify that parents go to extreme lengths to do things for us when we are too young to even 'notice', forget 'remember'. The Hong Kong trip was a great memory for my parents (nearly one-third of people visiting Disneyland are adults) and what singularly mattered to me then was the comfort and security of being with my parents, wherever they were.

It clearly means that plenty of painstaking efforts by parents to make us acquire knowledge and exclusive experiences do not matter in the long run.

The third finding of the ECLS states that there is a strong correlation between a child's performance and him having lots of books at home, but strangely, it doesn't matter much if his parents read to him nearly every day.

Having lots of books at home means having enough money to spend on books. Having a lot of books indicates educated and smart parents who encourage education and learning. The study says that having books is not a cause of intelligence but an indicator of intelligence.

Plenty of parents like you would have read bedtime stories to their children, night after night. Plenty of parents would have bought attractive books, month after month. Plenty of parents would have appreciated themselves for making their children intelligent. Let me share my experience. I have two writers at home. As a child, I felt that my parents loved books and newspapers more than me. It made me averse to books and reading for a long time. Though my parents enacted and read hundreds of stories to me, I did not enjoy it at all, maybe more so because they were trying too hard.

It clearly means that parents can enjoy their sleep without feeling guilty for not reading out a bedtime story every day to their bored children.

The study concludes that it isn't so much a matter of what you 'do' as a parent, it's who you 'are'. Parents work on children, like they do on projects. The important thing to understand is to work upon oneself rather than overzealously working upon the children.

How about staying a 'work in progress' parent who is inspired and informed to improve, not me but yourself. You need to whittle your ego to chisel the parent out of you. Trying relentlessly to chisel a perfect child will not work, not because you are not trying hard enough, but because you are trying too hard for something that does not depend entirely on you.

REASON 8

Tsunami of Social Media Messaging

My grandmother is an encyclopaedia of Indian TV shows. She would certainly get a perfect score in a SAT exam (if only there was one!) of viewing, analysing and reading about these shows. She recently told me about a new TV show which showed an 8-year-old boy marrying an 18-year-old girl. I laughed at the premise of the show, the same way I had laughed with her whenever I watched some of the other absurd shows full of naagins and heavily made-up witches. Then I heard my mother talking to other women who suddenly came together online to get the show banned.

I had never seen mothers getting so perturbed before with the regressive content of a TV show, which is the speciality of many high-TRP shows devoured by ardent female fans.

Subsequently, the serial was taken off air.[15] I have three questions in my mind.

Firstly, would these mothers have acted so swiftly and emotionally, had they been told to travel all the way to Mumbai and sign the petition? Most of them signed it because it was easy to go on a website and do it. Never before have they been so vocal about shows that have been abusing logic and sensibility for years. I understood—there was no social media to unite the reactivity of mothers then.

---

[15]http://timesofindia.indiatimes.com/tv/news/hindi/controversial-show-pehredaar-piya-ki-to-go-off-air/articleshow/60273159.cms

Secondly, when mothers know that children are impressionable, have they thought of giving a total miss to TV in their homes during their children's growing-up years? They created more buzz, more publicity around this regressive show through their show of solidarity. Did you try to declare at home not to watch this show at all rather than arguing to ban it? There are so many shows that your impressionable children are gobbling up and will continue to do so because their mothers or elder siblings are watching them.

Thirdly, do these mothers not see child abuse when they shed tears while watching talented children being pushed into competitive reality shows? When are they signing a petition to stop use of impressionable children in daily soaps, fashion shows, advertisements and reality shows?

A WhatsApp or FB revolution comes very handy for volatile parents to prove their parentability.

Though all adults love to gather information about relevant as well as irrelevant matters, parents take it one notch higher. They get bombarded by different kinds of information from various online platforms. These sensational nuggets influence parents more. Why?

Parents are a very anxious and fearful tribe. They start personalizing each turbulent piece as if it happened with their family.

Any mishap that happens anywhere on this earth shakes up my future plans.

When demonetisation shook up the world, my parents shook mine. 'What if she was alone somewhere with only thousand and five hundred rupee notes on that night?'

Really?

I was sitting in the same car as you, and you were reading

this news to me! And it is not like you would let me go out alone anyway. So who are we kidding?

We were watching a movie and the female lead was being fired for being late to work. My parents couldn't wait to get home to have a discussion and began in the theatre itself: 'What if this happens to her in the future? We all know how much she loves to sleep!'

Are. You. Kidding me?

I could not even comprehend the words that were being uttered and was only moments away from having steam coming out of my ears.

Parents also suffer from 'Sleeper Effect',[16] which means they get strongly impacted by a news piece even before its veracity or intent is established with certainty. They also forget the source of information but remember the information completely and clearly.[17]

My mother recently received a WhatsApp message with an image of the Indian flag hoisted atop the parliament of Israel for the first time.[18] She enthusiastically shared the photo with me. I could imagine the happy satisfaction and pride on her face as she would have pressed 'Forward' on her phone for contributing to my knowledge about international relations. I shared the rare gem of information in my 'Global Perspectives' class the next day. The teacher nodded with appreciation. For

---

[16]'Sleeper Effect': Psychologist Carl Hovland studied the impact of war movies, used as propaganda, on soldiers as well as masses.

[17]Also, the source of information fades faster than the information and its impact increases over time.

[18]https://www.thequint.com/news/india/image-indian-flag-israel-parliament-fake

the first time, I felt my mom's forwarded message forwarded my self-worth a bit in my class. The happiness was short-lived. My teacher returned the next day to announce that the picture was fake and I was yet another victim of the WhatsApp whirlwind.

> My mother had broken my trust.
> My mother had broken my heart.
> My mother had broken my reputation.
> Through just one message.

Though we know that the 'gyaan' delivered by WhatsApp messages cannot be trusted, we forget after a while whether we gathered the particular information from WhatsApp or Wikipedia or an advertisement. Our brain quickly forgets the source and only remembers the information and the holy family member who sent it to us at 6.23 a.m. The fake information gets circulated, shared, retweeted with a speed that allows reactions without reflection.

Any adult would believe the shared information, but the tribe of fearful parents escalate the issues exponentially if it even remotely concerns their children. Parents get outraged, get online support and the heat intensifies. Each class in school has a mothers' group which is always an emotionally charged battleground and breeding ground for escalating issues. 'Outrage is a really good way of getting your attention, because we don't choose outrage. It happens to us,' says design ethicist Tristan Harris.[19]

Parents, being vulnerable, easily share their outrage with other people. Adults, being vulnerable in the role of parents,

---

[19]https://www.ted.com/talks/tristan_harris_the_manipulative_tricks_tech_companies_use_to_capture_your_attention/transcript#t-90859

are more persuadable and fall prey to the automatic influence of social media networks.

How about not believing everything that every person claims to be true? How about not reading the orphaned information which is forwarded to you?

Social media activism only satisfies your thinking self but it makes you a 'passive parent'.

If a warrior enters the battleground, he can't shield himself from head to toe. That would reduce his agility and focus. He needs to master his defence skills.

It sucks how you think showing outrage on social media and 'creating' paper-thin daily digital revolutions to change the world will make you feel like an 'empowered complainer'. It would turn you into a change-maker at home. How about cutting the digital noise and growing time with us? How about giving up the television tsunami for creative hustling?

REASON 9

Awesome Wordsmiths, Awful Action-smiths

My mother has this fun-loving friend who survives on black coffee and her smartphone. Whenever we meet, she looks at me and tries to make a polite conversation, all the while tapping on her phone. She doesn't need to look at her phone while texting. What a talented woman!

The other day, she came to donate some books to the little library that I run in our society. With books also came two little boys.

'These are my sons,' she said matter-of-factly. I was more shocked than surprised as she didn't fit the 'mother' mould in my mind. I chatted with the acutely animated boys.

'My mom reads out stories to us every day,' said one.

'What did she read to you last night?' I asked.

'A story about a boy who was a lazy liar...'

'Like our mom...' said the other boy.

I froze there.

The younger boy went on innocently to share how they would get late for school every morning because Mommy dear over here would miss the alarm and then she would cook up a new story for being late.

I am amazed at you moms who permanently preach us to share our toys and toffees while you do not even share your yoga instructor's phone number with your friends.

You tell us to respect elders while you keep having cold wars and shouting matches with your brothers and sisters.

You are active online throughout the day but you expect us to stay away from this digital demon.

I meet this terrific aunty very often who sneaks sweets in her plate which her children do not let her eat as she is a diabetic. Yet, she loses her temper whenever her daughter misses her daily exercise regime. On top of it, on being confronted, she unabashedly explains that she repeatedly tells her daughter to exercise and eat less so that she can develop self-control. Parents defend their wrong actions by terming them as old habits which nobody guided them to break off at the right time.

'We are guiding you, making you aware so that you do not suffer like us,' is their defence stroke.

Parents forget that instructions and suggestions are mere word jugglery if not supported by suitable actions.

We can't tell others to speak gently while shouting at them. Can we?

There is a huge discrepancy between how you guys say you would behave and how you actually do.

Have you ever noticed why teaspoons keep disappearing from communal kitchens with surprising regularity?[20] The reason: people steal them. Have you ever noticed that girls trying clothes in fitting rooms always try to sneak in more dresses/clothes than what is allowed by the store? In USA, 85 per cent of shoppers try to take more than ten items for billing in the express lines which are specifically for those having ten times or less in the basket. In his research, Professor

---

[20]Richard Wiseman. 2008. *Quirkology: The Curious Science of Everyday Lives.* New York: Pan Macmillan. p. 221.

John Trinkaus[21] found that female van drivers were involved in far more antisocial behaviour, like breaking speed limits, parking in restricted areas, ignoring traffic signs, than their male counterparts.

In India, we find people fighting and shouting at the top of their voices at traffic signals and parking spaces. They start spitting anger much quicker and more intensely whenever any vehicle collision happens. Many of them, surely, are parents being watched by their children whom they preach to be polite.

Adults living in crowded, busy cities talk fast, walk fast and stress a lot. They look at their watches every few seconds. They suffer from 'sensory overload'.[22] They are so focused on their priorities because they are constantly bombarded with information from other people, their phones, traffic and advertising. They don't allow different things to catch their attention on roads. They walk past those who seek help. A majority of these adults surely are parents who must be doling out lessons to their children about being helpful and kind.

How are we expected to be kind, helping and caring towards strangers, elders and communities when our parents gift us

---

[21]John Trinkaus, professor at Zicklin School of Business in the City University of New York, studies ordinary people going about their everyday lives—a rich seam for quirkologic research.

[22]Stanley Milgram's research about 'sensory overload' in urban psychology, https://study.com/academy/lesson/urban-overload-hypothesis-lesson-quiz.html

watches to be checked every few seconds and running shoes to win every race?

Philip G. Zimbardo[23], a Professor and Psychologist at Stanford University, secretly filmed what happened when he left a car unlocked with its bonnet up on a street opposite the New York University. After just ten minutes, a passing car stopped and a family got out. The mother quickly removed anything of value from inside the car, the father removed the radiator with a hacksaw, whilst their child rooted through the boot. In broad daylight, the vehicle was raided by many people in the next few hours. We can imagine the same scenario happening in India, though there is no research pertaining to such behaviour.

How about trying to abstain from being saints in talk and sinners in walk? How about doing what you want us to do?

It sucks that parents promote 'idealism' in words, not in action. We only witness 'word models' in you, not role models.

---

[23]Wiseman, *Quirkology*, p. 259.

REASON 10

We Attract Conflict, You Shun Conflict

My classmate, a lead vocalist in a city band shared her experience. She was in the car with her family and the radio was playing a sad, 'would make you remember each heartbreak of your life' kind of a song.

'Dad, can you please change the channel?'

'Why? What's wrong with it?'

'It's a little depressing.'

'I like it.'

Since this was not going to end anytime soon, my friend quietly took her earphones out to listen to music on her phone. Within a few minutes, she heard faint noises on the car. She removed her earphones to realize the faint noises were actually her father screaming at the top of his lungs while her mother sported the most shocked look on her face because of whatever was happening.

'You can't even listen to a song that your father wants to listen to. If you defy your father in such small things, I can very well imagine what you will do next.'

'But…'

'What but? Who do you think you are? Have you become this old that you cannot obey your father? And how many times have I told you that these earphones of yours are not good and they will reduce your hearing ability?'

'She only uses them in the car,' her mother tried to diffuse the heightened tension.

'Rather than telling her not to use earphones, you are teaching her to defy and argue with her own father.'

'*Arre...*'

'No more discussion. Fine. Just listen to whatever you want.'

My friend was incredibly angry and hurt upon reaching their destination.

And guess what the father did next...

Yes, many of you probably guessed right. The father acted as if nothing had happened.

When it comes to conflict, we are either conflict seekers or conflict avoiders.

For instance, my cousin is a permanent conflict seeker. He keeps sending friend requests to arguments and conflicts of all shapes and sizes! Once, he wanted to colour his hair golden and get a small tattoo. He had made all his plans in his head, from finalizing the shade of the hair highlights to the tattoo design. His grand plan came crashing when his mother, with whom he had shared it all, could not muster the courage to share it with his dad. When my friend tried to convince his father, he screamed: 'No playing around with your body and my money.'

No means no.

You might be a conflict seeker at your workplace but you may turn into a conflict avoiding parent at home. You allow the dissent to simmer without looking for a solution because it hurts to negotiate or even discuss with someone you gave birth to. You try everything to ignore having a disagreement or a defiant stance from someone you nurtured.

Since conflict is a permanent part of growing up, it raises its ugly but inevitable head every now and then. As we grow, we attract conflict and you try your hardest to ignore it. You primarily use your authority to silence any conflict raging in our hearts. You expect us to be listening champions with dormant debating skills while your listening skills hibernate in front of us.

If our latent arguments become active, you argue and threaten, intensely. If our disagreement persists, you sulk and self-loathe, extensively. Either you surrender dramatically or you expect us to kneel down. Why is it complete victory or total loss that you orchestrate through a conflict? Why can't there be a middle ground where both the parties understand and respect each other's opinions?

You guys use your 'authority' to push us into submission. You guys think of authority as a response to our disobedience: we act up, you crack down. Have you ever thought the other way round? The disobedience/disagreement could be a response to your authority. If the parent will not do his job properly, the child will become disobedient.[26]

'When people in authority want the rest of us to behave, it matters—first and foremost—how they behave,' says Malcolm Gladwell in his book *David & Goliath*.[24]

This is called the 'Principle of Legitimacy', and legitimacy is based on three things:

- The people who are asked to obey authority have to feel like they have a voice—that if they speak up, they will be heard.
- The law has to be predictable and there has to be a reasonable expectation that the rules tomorrow are going to be roughly the same as the rules today.

---

[24]Malcolm Gladwell shares his thoughts in the context of teachers in his book, *David & Goliath*. In my opinion, it is equally true for parents. Malcom Gladwell. 2013. *David & Goliath*. Boston: Little, Brown and Company. p. 206.

- The authority has to be fair and cannot treat one group differently.

Though he believes that all good parents know these three principles implicitly, I have some major doubts here. Are we genuinely heard when we speak up? My friend trying to listen to music in the car doesn't think so. The rules formed by parents are so arbitrary that they change with their moods. How are we supposed to sway along? When it comes to fairness, most of the respondents to my survey mentioned that they are treated differently from their siblings.

A 16-year-old jumped from his flat in a high-rise and ended his life and everyone, including the parents, was shocked and surprised. Did he never say things like, 'I don't know what to do'? Did he never share—even in hushed tones—trouble brewing in school or some relationship? Did he never try to reach out?

When I try to send across the message that I can't handle it alone, you seem to trivialize it by deflecting attention. You develop your problem-avoidance mechanisms—denial, scapegoating, blaming authority or character assassination.

'My Child was not depressed.' —Denial

'It happened as another batchmate did the same.' —Scapegoating

'The school authorities were inhumanly competitive.' —Blaming authority

'It must have been because of some girl he was with.' —Character Assassination

It is possible that his parents thought that suicide, like cancer, happens to other people only.

They took all his troubles as a phase. They might have said,

'We never thought it to be so serious.' Surprisingly, parents are also guilty, to some extent, of turning India into a teenage suicide hotspot.[25]

On the other hand are musing moms who blow the warning signal for every minute incident. If a teacher snaps at your child in the class and he mentions it to you, a WhatsApp wave might hit all the parents leading to a temperamental tsunami by next morning. You choose to fight non-existent battles.

Watch out for the stone because we never get hit by a mountain. A mountain being huge is easily visible but is not always the problem. Choosing the right battles and fighting them at the ripe moment is difficult but needed.

Why is it that you roll your sleeves and jump right into the situation when the only thing I want is an empathetic ear? Why is it that you merely nod and offer a surficial, verbal fix when what I yearned for was your active involvement in my problem?

Next time, when you have the urge to ignore or blow up a conflict, please observe us silently, closely, passionately, regularly and honestly. Silently, because we can listen to the heartfelt truth in silence. Closely, because sometimes there is more distance between two rooms than between cities. Passionately, because parenting can be a pain and you might slip when you need to hang on the most. Regularly, because your children change faster than the next phone software. Honestly, because you might

---

[25]https://moonparenting.wordpress.com/2016/06/16/a-suicide-hotbed-called-india/

be tempted to deny seeing the real child as compared to your 'dream child.'

How about talking about our problems without bringing our relationship in between? Could you speak to me without bruising my self-esteem or nursing an ego wound? Could we seek each other out with an intention to build new bridges of flexibility and friendship for the future?

REASON 11

My Children Are Mine Only

My friend and I joined a dog lovers club—POOCH—which feeds stray dogs. Since we fed biscuits to some of the dogs outside my building compound for a few days, some of them started entering into the premises. A senior resident complained to my friend's mother. 'Your child's habit is spoiling our morning walk. These stray dogs enter the compound searching for him, whom I have seen feeding them.'

His mother had to hear these hard-hitting words in front of the other residents. She got so angry with those dogs and her son that she retorted, 'Did the dog ask you about my son? How can you blame him like this?'

Once his mother reached home, her tongue cut my friend into the tiniest of pieces as she dared him to ever go close to any kind of dog. She also decided to sever all ties with the complaining aunty.

You love to hate us, criticize us and admonish us at any hour of the day. But you do not know how to handle it when someone else merely attempts to mention something against us. When someone criticizes us, you take it personally. You consider it as a criticism of your parenting. You take it as your failure and it becomes insulting and hurtful. You love us, but you really, really love yourself. We, extensions of your image, flag-bearers of your public persona, belong to you and only you—our protectors and saviours.

To counter any such 'giving bad press' attempt by any

friend, relative or acquaintance, you guys resort to either of these two strategies:

- You scrape to the bottom of the barrel of our personalities to serve all possible positives present in us.

  While leaving for our hometown to celebrate Diwali, my mother handed over all our plant pots to the nursery in-charge of our society. Among other plants, there were two tiny pots of exotic plants. Since they were gifts, she instructed him to take special care of those two. And just like any predictable Hindi film, one of the tiny pots went missing. The in-charge apologized profusely and promised to find the thief. He checked the CCTV footage and saw a young boy casually picking the pot and walking towards the lift. My mother knew the father of the culprit as they both happened to be on one of the society committees.

  The nursery in-charge spoke to the gentleman about his son. He gave back the pot with a wilted plant in it. We got the plant. My mother expected an apology from the boy. It never came.

  The gentleman met my mother a few days later. After the mandatory small talk, he casually mentioned, '*Arre*, my son is a real plant lover. He liked that pot in the nursery and brought it home. You know how these kids are—so busy with studies that he forgot to water it also. He was so sorry for what he did. I told him that I will get another plant for Aunty. Only then, he felt better.'

  The twist in the tale was that the nursery in-charge had

already told us that the father had scolded his son badly while returning him the pot. However, he shielded his son with all his might in front of my mother!

You never acknowledge our mistakes or faults in front of others because it makes you feel small, imperfect and inadequate. You try to spin it into a positive trait somehow, or you whip up a quick excuse.

- The second stratagem is 'attack is the best defence', which my friend's mother had used with the senior residents. Had my mom faced the wrath of those residents due to my association with POOCH, she would have portrayed me as a hard-core dog lover. She would have turned the tables by labelling the senior residents as 'animal haters' who were trying to label me, an animal welfare activist, as a 'miscreant disturbing their morning walk'.

When you pass the parcel of criticism to us, it becomes about us. We are failing you by bringing such criticism to your doorstep.

Your anger becomes layered by the time you reach us—the real reason behind your wrath. The first layer of anger is caused by those friends who got an opportunity to say something disturbing to you.

It is covered by another layer of anger caused by the action of that child who is known as yours.

Layer one: How dare the friend say so?

Layer two: How dare my son/daughter do so?

The layered anger works slowly on us, turning us into a delicious dish cooked slowly on the flames of anger. We are marinated by your sharp words, then tempered with reminders of some previous wrongdoings before shutting the lid with some prohibitive punishment.

The nicer you talk in front of others, the angrier you get in front of us.

Parents reserve the right of fault-finding, criticizing and nagging their children. They would never trade it off for anything.

'Good or bad, mean or sensible, they are our children' is their credo.

Since you shield us from criticism aimed by the world towards us, we do not know how to handle it later when you are not the 'Great Wall of China' between us and the world. We just block out those people who think differently. We keep emitting emotional responses like you did.

Since you blast us up for everything, we ignore it. Since you do not let others pick at us, we do not learn resilience. We become socially awkward.

How about being fair and letting us face the valid criticism with positivity? How about not running to save us from falling down but help us in standing up?

REASON 12

Claimers and Blamers

Whenever I did well in an exam, got a positive remark over an assignment or received some award, my mother would congratulate and hug me, and then drop the bomb—'You're welcome'. It always came as a reminder for me to say 'Thank you' to her.

I agree that she would have certainly helped me, directly or indirectly, in doing well in that exam or assignment. But the instantaneous 'claiming for credit' unsettles me.

And, whenever I underperformed in an exam or got a negative remark over an assignment, my mother would hug and say some motivational words, and then drop many bombs— 'You did not work hard enough', 'You don't focus these days', 'You don't listen to me'.

The shrapnel of these blame bombs wound me.

I joke with her sometimes that her first words to me after my birth would surely have been, 'You're welcome', not to offer a real welcome but to wriggle out a 'Thank you'—from a newborn!

If I fall sick, I am to be blamed.

If I feel better, she is to be thanked.

Parents suck because they are such unfair allocators of blame and credit. They over-claim the credit to themselves and over-allocate the blame to children.

Though most human beings feel that they always contribute more than the rest in their personal and professional chores, this over-claiming reaches another level when it comes to married couples and single parents. Married couples have 'multi-level over-claiming'. The first level is used to outshine the contribution of the significant other. A wife always believes and reiterates that the husband's help in the household is as miniscule as the amount of spices in a patient's diet. A husband, on the other hand, tries to prove how extremely busy and stressed he is at work. He tries hard to prove that he bears all the important responsibilities at work amidst a group of non-performers.

The second level of over-claiming is used by the couple or single parent to take credit equalling Mount Everest at parenting. They see and feel so intensely about what they do as parents that their brains fail to register what others do or what they do in other roles.

You guys suffer from egocentrism. It simply means that you are too focused on your own thoughts and actions as Mom or Dad, while paying no attention to what the other half of the equation is doing.

You allocate blame to others and credit to yourself in raising us because:

- Every person honestly believes that his/her contribution in terms of emotional, mental and material involvement is more. Every mother and father feels that they never get their due as parents. They always feel that their efforts are undervalued and under-respected. Each Mom and Dad feels that they have sacrificed a huge chunk of their lives to raise their children. You repeatedly point it to us and, at times I feel like asking you, 'Didn't YOU choose to be a parent?'
- Mothers suffer from this phenomenon more because

they spend more time with children on a daily basis for almost two decades. Many mothers tweak their work schedules or give up professional engagements to focus on their 'mother' job. Though we might not be appreciating or needing your presence and involvement to that level, your heightened claim for credit happens because you pay a huge price in your head.

- Parents who go horribly wrong in their upbringing attempt also try to claim that they did their best. They easily blame the factors outside their control—economy, a family member or the child himself. Sometimes, they simply refuse to admit their mistakes. Sometimes, they blame it on others for damage control, and sometimes they actually believe that they are innocent. Hence, they turn defensive. The reasons for their 'raising attempt gone wrong' may be different, the casualty remains the same—US.

- Parents over-claim in their parenting role because it is the pivot of their lives. They over-claim as their ideal self tells them to always keep their parenting hat at the top, to give it the prime slot of their life show. My mother would repetitively remind me about my classes, due dates of submissions, more to prove to herself than to me that that she is playing her 'mother role' to perfection. Later on, she would claim the credit for all my good performances and blame me for any shortcomings.

'You succeeded in XYZ because of my alertness and timely advice, else you would have failed in XYZ the way you messed up in ABC.'

I know Mom, you are 110 per cent responsible for all that goes right in my life. But that's what you think. If I go and ask Dad about his contribution in making me who I am, your collective contribution will certainly be more than 130 per cent![26]

That is logic-defying, but you, being the centre of your own world, have an unbeatable Mummy logic.

I thought you could motivate me to do better by not proving how awesome you are, but by showing how awesome I am.

Parents expect gratitude every hour. They want their efforts to be noticed, they expect their emotional investment in their children to be valued and suitably reciprocated.

Parents label their children as 'thankless and ungrateful' all the time because the amount of gratitude shown by children towards their parents is always less than their expectations.

How about being fair as a human being? How about not being a hungry credit-seeker?

Parents blame children blatantly because they are easy targets and their argument arsenal is miniscule in front of the large ego chambers of parents.

How about renouncing the seniority and authority tag while counting all that you have done for your children? There is

---

[26]Individuals tend to overestimate their relative contributions to collaborative endeavours. Thus, the sum of group member estimates of the percentage they each contributed to a joint task typically exceeds the logically allowable 100%.
Nicholas Epley, professor of behavioural science at Booth School of Business, talks about this concept in the book, *Economic Growth: Theories and Policies Vs Evidence*.

no seniority here—If I am 16, you are my 16-year-old 'Mom'.

As soon as one asks for 'being grateful' or 'being thankful', it loses its purity, sanctity and power.

Gratitude cannot be demanded like explanations. Blame cannot be doled out like freebies.

I acutely agree that parents are the most giving creatures. No one would ever do for us what they do. But their constant referring and reminding takes away the austere magnificence.

REASON 13

Intention, Intention Go Away, Outcome Is Here to Stay

You like my X classmate very much because he tops the class. You appreciate our neighbours because both their daughters are doctors. You 'used' to appreciate your friends, Mrs Y and Mr Z, as their two sons studied at the Indian Institute of Technology (IIT) but now both of them have started a company to offer water conservation solutions to farmers. IITian turned social entrepreneur is not a very impressive outcome for you. 'Exceptional education' is a preferred outcome only till we study and 'exceptional income' is the next preferred and expected outcome.

Our intentions are like the ads on digital media which you can skip in '3, 2, 1... seconds', and outcomes are the real content. Your definition of success expects us to get power, money and fame in any order.

Though you realize that the rich, powerful or famous status of a person is not entirely of his making, you still base his valuation on his monetary, fame or power index.

There are many sensible decisions which end up having unlucky outcomes. Many films, like *Andaz Apna Apna*, *Lamhe* or *Rockstar*, even with their unique storylines, amazing cast and moving music, fail. Most of the academic toppers do not top every test of life. They do not change the world. Marriage of two extremely successful and compatible individuals crumbles.

You guys judge those decisions more harshly of which

you were not a part of. You condemn a failed outcome of our efforts very harshly if you did not approve of it in the first place. 'We told you so', 'We always knew it' are the standard responses when what we need would be an empathetic pat or an honest analysis of our intentions.

It is very easy to label a decision 'wrong' once the outcome or end result is negative. It seems that you wait for that decision to go wrong and then shoot all your arrows in that direction with the finesse of Deepika Kumari.[27] When I want to lick my wounds amidst silent tears, you would put the final nail in the coffin: 'Dekha, when you are in pain, even we suffer'.

Is there any sane being around who could tell you that I am suffering because you are inflicting the pain?

Have you heard about the word 'journey'? I know 'destination' comes much before it in the dictionary.

Your love for the end result makes us focus only on the destination and not the journey.

It erases the thin line between ethical and unethical as we develop a 'whatever it takes' attitude.

When minor immoral actions of ours are ignored by you as there is no immediate harmful impact, it becomes too late to intervene when major dangerous outcomes raise their ugly heads. Cancer survivor and seven-time Tour de France winner, cyclist Lance Armstrong, became the most celebrated and inspiring sportsman until he fell from grace when he was proven guilty of taking performance-enhancing drugs.[28] Love

---

[27]Deepika Kumari is an Indian athlete who competes in archery and is currently ranked in top 10 archers of the world.
[28]https://www.theguardian.com/sport/2013/aug/13/alex-rodriguez-lance-armstrong-cheaters

for outcomes makes people do things that they repent forever.

When I make a pleading face to get more time to play a video game or watch two more episodes of the latest Web series, my intention is to breach the norm and take you for a ride. You let me do it. When I help my inebriated friend reach home safely, my intention is to apologize to you for reaching home late but your anger blurs my intention. The 'why' behind the 'what' goes unnoticed.

If you judge my transgression solely by outcome, you will turn me into a manipulator.

Not only outcomes, you love 'measureable' outcomes, like:

- Which grade are you in?
- How old are you?
- How many prizes, championships and scholarships have you won?
- How many classes, summer programmes and internships have you applied for?
- How many job offers?
- What are the packages?

Parents love objectivity while speaking to other children. Numbers impress them. Famous names impress them. Every quantifiable achievement is a real accomplishment to form a perception about the child under their scanner. Parents love to measure the success by stressing on the percentage and percentile secured, admission offers received, countries visited and cars bought.

You feel more pride in sharing the numbers than sharing our virtues that cannot be measured.

When I entered Class VI, I moved to a new school. In our first surprise Maths test, I kept staring at the questions as if they will have mercy on me and give answers on their own. Other students managed to ask each other and scored well. For me, I got less marks because I was honest. For my mom, I got less marks. Period.

Measureable outcomes sweep parents off their feet. Since success stories with real measureable outcomes are reported by online and offline media in abundance, it gives out a false belief that it happens often and easily.

We start expecting measureable outcomes falling in our laps like a six-figure salary, a successful start-up, TV interviews, a deal to host a show or write a column.

Seven hundred likes, 1,436 profile views in a week, fifteen retweets—all these add to our love for measured outcomes.

If they are told that their child can apply either for an annual scholarship of ₹25,000 or a one-time scholarship of ₹5 lakh, they would be more excited for the latter. When they are told that around hundred students will apply for the latter, the excitement remains the same because they are influenced by the magnitude of the outcome, not its likelihood. Though this is true of all adults, parents fall for it more often because the heart beats the head big time.

Parents love exclusivity. They attach extra value to those things which are scarce. Just as your heart jumps up to acquire a piece of furniture as soon as the website displays a 'sold out' sign over it, you desperately want us to participate in an event if only one seat is left.[29]

---

[29]Principle of Scarcity is a major persuasive tool, to influence buying behaviour of consumers, according to professor of psychology and marketing, Robert Cialdini.

If life stories of people like Azim Premji or Smriti Irani impress you, please do not run behind us for that one mark or that one degree.

People who really know us would be aware of our intentions. Parents know it when we burn that extra midnight oil or sweat it out like a maniac. Despite these efforts, we could mess up on that test or game.

When organizers, audience, teachers and fellow students clap for winners, it makes sense. They cannot value our efforts. But when you feel disappointed by our performance and fail to 'factor in' our intentions, it feels bizarre.

Since you are the only one who know about the making of the film of our lives, you should value our 'unsung' efforts despite the presence of the 'hero' outcome. If you guys stand by us in the wake of failed outcomes, our spirits will never fail.

Should you ruthlessly proclaim: 'The world only sees the outcome'? How about giving us the right perspective to welcome failure and value lessons from outcomes?

How about enjoying our journeys with us without being judgemental about the result? How about encouraging us to give our best and forget the rest?

REASON 14

Halo Effect

An 11-year-old shared his predicament with me: 'A family has just relocated from New Zealand in the neighbourhood. The family members are well-built and impeccably dressed at all times. Quite impressed by the "picture-perfect" family, my mother talks to them every day and appreciates their children all the time. She likes everything about this family these days.

'The new neighbour told us that they eat at least six fruits every day and a sixty-minute walk is a fixed part of their daily routine.'

I told the boy about 'Halo Effect'.[30] I laughingly suggested to my young friend that their fruit intake and exercising is going to rise in the coming days because his mother will get 'anchored' by whatever the neighbour is saying. She will be primed to offer more number of fruits to her family. She will coerce each member of her family to dress well and walk daily. If some of them were already exercising, she will nudge them to do more.

This is how parents get influenced by anyone whom they get impressed with. My parents always have a specimen available for conducting any experiment, i.e. me, and so I receive sudden bouts of more fruits in my diet and health-improvement tips.

---

[30] The Halo Effect is a type of cognitive bias in which our overall impression of a person influences how we feel and think about his or her character.

One quality of a person—fame, riches or academic achievement—catches your attention and creates a permanent positive impression in your minds.

You put a halo around young achievers.

'Look at Sania Mirza', 'Look at the topper of your class'. 'Be like them'.

Ok. I am looking at Sania. Her dad was a passionate sportsperson and accompanied her to all her tournaments. You didn't even take me to the neighbourhood park.

I have grown up watching your passion for watching TV and playing Candy Crush.

You get impressed by many children except your own. Each child is a 'red moon' when you talk to us. They appear more polite, far more talented and better looking than they actually are.

Yet, I become a 'powerhouse of talent' when you appreciate me in my absence. I fail to understand what is your true opinion about me and others?

My mother came to my school and (unfortunately for me) met some fellow parents. This is how she replayed the experience for me:

'Asha's daughter made such a beautiful painting for her birthday.'

'I met your classmate A's father and he was praising his son's time-management skills. He said that A has become very fit.' (She even praises their pets in front of me!)

What I come to know later is a completely different story. Asha Aunty got gallons of gyan about my singing prowess from my mom. 'A' told me the next day how my mom was going gaga about my Rubik's cube talent and how I had never missed school in the whole year.

When parents like something or someone, they like everything about them. When they like themselves, they like everything about themselves. When they do not like my friend, they hate everything about her including her surname. My mom loves Mr Bachchan and hence we buy jewellery only from Tanishq (the brand he endorses). Since she has no particular liking for Parineeti Chopra, Kurkure is not welcome at our place.

You get primed and we bear the brunt.

You prime us too.

If I hear a sentence like, 'Would you pass and get about 50 per cent?' before every result, I would be primed to think like someone who could merely pass.

If I hear a sentence like, 'Would you get about 90 per cent?' I would be primed to think like someone who would score about 90 per cent.

'Being a parent' primes our moms and dads to become more righteous. A research proved that 'being a parent' affects moral evaluation of harmless but offensive acts.[31]

Whatever was acceptable to you when you were not a parent becomes heinous after you become a Mom or Dad. As a teenager, breaking curfew sometimes was fine with you, but now you are a mighty moral mom who gives terrible headaches to us. Every parent uses a halo of morality like a hula hoop.

How about being fair in your assessment of others as well as your own children? How about not being overly moral after wearing the parent hat?

---

[31] https://www.researchgate.net/publication/256752675_Priming_family_values_How_being_a_parent_affects_moral_evaluations_of_harmless_but_offensive_acts

My friend recently told me how she uses the Halo Effect to her advantage: 'My mother judges all my friends as soon as she sees them. I tell all my friends who come home to upload an excited "Namaste Aunty" as soon as they spot my mother. Then I casually but deliberately add, "Mum, X topped the Maths test".

'When she asks, "X, what would you like to have?" I add that X loves my tiffin every day.

'For my mother, a girl who loves Maths and her food is always welcome in the house.'

'Halo' means glory. Parents have a glorified perception of themselves. They always believe that they are doing everything perfect as parents. How about being a little more authentic?

At the same time, they like to believe that their children are the most ungrateful, impolite and sluggish people while all the other children are syrupy-sweet characters out of Sooraj Barjatya films. Parents form a skewed general perception based on any one good or bad quality in a child. How about being more rational and less biased towards children?

All of these emotions are exaggerated versions of reality but parents stick to them the way sauce sticks to pasta in a delicious fettuccine arrabiata. Parents feel very sure of their thoughts and opinions as parents. This surely makes them rigid and inflexible.

How about being more open in accepting change and less fixated with what you think is right?

REASON 15

I Act, Therefore I Am

Consider two situations:

X: Paul owns shares in Company A. In the past year, he considered switching his stock to Company B, but he decided against it. He now learns that he would have been better off by $1,200, if he had switched.

Y: George owned shares in Company B. In the past year, he switched his stock to Company A. He now learns that he would have been better off by $1,200 had he stayed with Company B.

Who feels greater regret?

Daniel Kahneman uses this example in his famous book, *Thinking, fast and slow*,[32] to inform that 8 per cent of respondents said X while 92 per cent said Y.

In our case, though both the parents are economically in a similar situation, Parent X reached here by not acting while Parent Y reached here by taking action.

We feel intense emotions when we take action. Mothers, in order to feel relevant while contributing to their 'mother' job, try to remain in action all the time. They love to appear busy.

A friend of mine is tired of her mother's promptness in attending every school meeting, replying to every email, meeting career counsellors and reading numerous articles on

---

[32]Daniel Kahneman. 2011. *Thinking, fast and slow*. New York: Penguin. p. 348.

endless topics and sharing them with her.

'She has taken a sabbatical for me and my younger brother. She is all out to prove it to herself and the world that she did the right thing as "being a mother" is keeping her "in action",' said my friend.

Parents love to stay in action—physically by running errands and make things available to their children; and on the verbal front, they love supplying advice, instruction, appreciation or criticism.

You use constant advising to prove that you know a lot and are serious about helping us. You don't hesitate from constant criticism when you feel that you are putting in more efforts in us as compared to the improvement shown by us.

I think every generation has a 'good mother' stereotype that is promptly promoted like a pinned post on your generation page. For my grandmom's generation, this stereotype meant being undemanding and silently giving. A good mother would have no story of her own but would narrate stories of others.

And the 'good mother' stereotype for my mother's generation means being a former achiever who prioritizes her responsibilities and is exceptionally adaptive. Sacrifice and flexibility are programmed in a mother's code.

Our mothers try harder to play to the gallery because their 'good mother' stereotype demands more from them: They should either be supermoms who balance their domestic and professional lives like a gymnast or they should be fully flexible to shun the professional limelight and accept the domestic garb.

Each mom wants to sacrifice something to prove that she is a good mother. She feels guilty if she enjoys her work more than her kids. I don't understand how a majority of women slip effortlessly into the 'good mother' stereotype.

Recently, a very dear student of my Mom came to visit her after a decade. She had just had her second baby. She told my Mom that she did not feel any special emotion or surge of love when her first child was born. 'I kept waiting to feel something out of the world, but nothing happened. The first year was really tiring. My house was such a mess all the time that I decided to have my second child quickly so that I would be done with this mess once and for all. I wanted to return to having a clean home again.'

I laughed with her when she said so because it was honest and pragmatic.

Moms suck when they become OTT (over the top) moms. They suck when 'stress' is their default mode and it pushes them to be 'in action' mindlessly. Many children complain that the most annoying thing about their moms is that they take too much stress, which then trickles down to them.

Harvard professor Kathleen McGinn says that daughters of working mothers earned more, had better jobs and studied better, while the sons were more sensitive and gave time to childcare.

So, even experts believe that your going outside for work helps us in performing better at school, which in turn improves our chances of a better future. Your working also reduces gender inequality at home.

Then why do you wish to stay at home and channelize all your energy and talent towards raising us.

My mom is guilty of doing the same on many occasions.

One weekend, we both went to a café. The ultra-smiling, enthusiastic waiter came with the menu and started explaining it. I told him that we will read it but he went on to explain the 'dish of the day' sheet positioned on our table. I flipped through it and thanked him.

'He resembles you.' I told Mom.

Message delivered. No damage reported.

Parents need to be mindful of their actions.

Playing to a set stereotype of 'informed-involved' mom is more hurtful than helpful. I am not at all negating the immensely helpful guidance of mothers in our growing up years. I am merely concerned about the excessive support.

Talented, well-educated mothers choose to leave the workforce to become 'full-time mothers'. Claiming that most day-care facilities are nightmares, they stick to their homebound status. In order to channelize their energy and reduce the frustration of losing financial independence, they end up getting extra involved with raising their children. How about taking up some course to keep your minds occupied?

Please keep your parenthood in perspective. Getting loads of educational toys aimed at sharpening various skills, driving children to daily classes, helping them in homework is going 'over the top'. How about being an 'observer' and not a 'player'?

Your presence is more valuable than your actions. Please do not try to prove your utility. Your being there as an emotional anchor and an empathetic friend is more important than your frenetic efforts to add tangible value.

REASON 16

Paper or Plastic, or Both

Have you heard of the Japanese dining concept of Omakase, where the diners let the chef choose their order and decide the dishes to be served?

Omakase translates to, 'I'll leave it to you', and it makes diners happy because they get their meal as a surprise. But it puts tremendous pressure on the chefs to come up with innovative and delicious preparations appealing to the diner's senses.

Parents try to be Omakase chefs every day, which is an impossible feat to achieve. We do not want a surprise meal every day. Moreover, we will be expected to appreciate it nonetheless.

You guys want to make all the decisions for us—may be because you are older than us, or you believe that you know more, or because you certainly believe that you have more experience than us and you love to believe that you know what is good for us.

If you had more children, you would have needed to take so many more decisions. But because you decided to have one or two kids, you must be making fewer decisions. Hell, no!

Your decision-making mechanism sucks because:

- **You love options more than us**. My child needs a new water bottle. Search. My child should go to a small preparatory session before pre-school. Search. These searches multiplied by online reviews and offline suggestions produce a mammoth selection to feast on. The problem is: The more the number of choices, the more inner paralysis we suffer from.[33] You want to prove it to yourself that you have been that perfect parent who has given all the possible choices to his/her children. You are proud of yourself for spending sleepless nights diving in the sea of choices to excitedly come up with new ones each time. Your need to be the best possible friend, philosopher and guide pushes you to become a 'search specialist'. You guys are more intensely micromanaging the lives of those one or two offerings you have decided to give birth to. As you desperately want to be a part of your children's lives forever, you try to contribute by landing into every possible decision with your barrage of options.

- **You love to keep options open**. Though the confusion is killing you and making you unhappy, you still want us to experience the 'best of everything', which eventually turns out to be a 'best of nothing'. Parents overconfidently believe that they know what would be best for their kid's future. They certainly think that they know what will make their kids happy, which is sheer nonsense. Dan Gilbert, the professor of 'Happiness' conducted an experiment.[34] In a photography class at Harvard, two groups of students were asked to choose two photographs each. They were asked to

---

[33] Psychologist Barry Scwartz says so in his 2004 book, *Paradox of Choice* (HarperCollins, p. 147).
[34] https://www.youtube.com/watch?v=4q1dgn_C0AU

give one photograph to the teacher while keeping one with them. Only one group was told that they could change their choice of photographs after a few days. The students who had the flexibility of exchanging the pictures were really displeased with their choices. They didn't like the photos that they had kept with themselves as much as the group which had no option to change. This is how 'open options' rob us off our happiness. This is how parents keep offering options to us and keep snatching happiness and pleasure from us.

- **You love to make almost every decision for us.** You feel obligated to be a part of each decision that impacts our life. You think that we would make mistakes in making decisions because we are inexperienced, gullible and dreamy. You want to be our SAFETY NETS to save us from all potential threats. And that creates a problem—Your making decisions for us does not equip us to make decisions in the future.

You think too much because you are a 'chronic over-thinker'!

'I don't have money. How do I give them the best education?'

'I have so much money, how do I stop them from getting spoiled?'

Just like it is believed that every tasty eatable would be harmful for health, parents believe that anything that kids enjoy would be detrimental for them. Anything 'fun' is 'harmful'.

'Should I let him watch TV?'

'Should I let him watch for as long as one hour?'

'Should I let him watch *Shin Chan*?'

'Can I let him laugh while he watches silly scenes?'
'Shouldn't he be playing outdoors?'
'Is it safe?'
'Which sport should he play?'
'Should I search about...'
Oh Lord, please tell your 'thinking tanker' to stop.

We make better, proper decisions with a less range of selection. It is so difficult to administer our selection criteria to a large group. It stresses us and leads to discontent.

How about prioritizing areas which actually need options? I will be fine with any water bottle as long as it can store water for a few hours.

How about observing me more closely than the search result so that you can convert the long list into a shorter one?

I love all the colours and the brands of water bottles. I would want them all. I will cry and pester you to buy me all. I will be dissatisfied and angry even when you buy me two (when I need one) because you haven't bought me the rest.

Please don't obsess over options. You seek out all the possible additional information about best schools/colleges or buying a new product before making a decision. Even when additional information merely wastes time and money and adds to the confusion, it comforts you that you worked hard before making an important decision.

We must learn to close doors, to sacrifice options. Don't keep all the doors open, even if the handle turns effortlessly. Extra information just creates 'illusion of knowledge.'

How about sitting with us and listening to what we want to do with our lives? How about sticking to minimum facts and taking apt decisions before drowning ourselves into the sea of information?

REASON 17

Opinion Overdose

- Finish your homework right now.
- Best option for you is to finish your homework right now.
- It is always better to finish homework as soon as possible.
- I used to finish my homework before anything else.
- I thought you would finish your homework first.

These are five different prescriptions used by different parents for their children. The way doctors assess whether the patient is responding to their prescribed medicines or not, parents also check whether children are responding to their verbal histrionics or not.

If the response is not encouraging, doctors, as well as parents, try different combinations.

Parents start with the first option which is an *Instruction* (Finish your homework right now). They begin with the use of authority, by instructing us to do a specific task. If the instruction is followed, they remain in authority mode. If not, they step down to the use of *Advice* (Best option for you is to finish your homework right now). It is a direct way of telling the child to finish his homework immediately, also hinting at the consequences of not paying attention to the advice. This is a manipulative mode for parents to achieve the desired action from their children.

If the children do not respond well to advice, parents step

down further towards *Suggestion* (It is always better to finish homework as soon as possible). It is an indirect, idea-like recommendation which is conventionally accepted. Suggestions are neutral and not intense. However, if the children remain unaffected by suggestions, too, then the parents try out an '*Opinion*' (I used to finish my homework before anything else). It is a loose adaptation of one's general viewpoint. It is a 'spineless' suggestion, 'muted' advice and 'dubbed' instruction.

In the end, if all the verbal weaponry fails to evoke the desired response from children, parents give it a final try in the form of an *Expectation* from children (I thought you would finish your homework first).

Parents never shy away from trying different options at different times. They put all the patience present in them to good use to influence children to buy their viewpoint.

My survey respondents agreed in unison that all parents have these annoying habits: Repetition camouflaged as Instructions (sometimes threats), Advice (sometimes real-life examples), Suggestions (sometimes statistical), Opinions (mostly overconfident overdose of personal and imaginary experiences) and Expectations (always traumatic).

'I feel like a bird being lectured about how to fly,' wrote one.

'Sometimes, I worry about my mother's vocal chords. They are in constant workout mode,' wrote another.

When I think about their constant effort to be of some help to us, it seems like a producer–director team working on a film. Though the duo has hired a whole team to take care of all the aspects of film-making, they are always anxious. They monitor more than what is needed, they use their authority to make everyone work according to their vision, they advice storywriters based on social suggestions and previous success stories and they suggest too many possibilities based on their personal experiences (which is very vast in their opinion).

The only problem is that a film is not a human being like us. It is a creation brought to life for others. Children cannot be treated similarly.

Parents constantly instruct, advice, suggest, opine and expect because:

- They are always under pressure to perform.
- They are scared of the uncertain future. So they rant, roar and repeat. We do not listen because the overdose kills us.
- They want us to be their 'best achievements'. Everything is fair in 'love for children' and 'war against future'.

Elections are contested and won, interviews are cracked—achievements made not on the basis of facts, but on feelings. We all love information from different sources but we forget to sieve facts from opinions. Facts are fixed, facts are few and facts are bland and boring. Opinions are many, opinions are malleable and opinions can be irrational and ignorant. Based on an overdose of opinions from online and offline orators, parents become an advice-churning machine.

Moms are magnets of opinions, they attract opinions from all over. Though they never believe us, they will believe whatever these self-confessed authorities mumble. It is like following one of those celebrities who is a yoga expert one weekend, diet expert the next weekend and then she would be seen modelling for sweat absorbing/repelling fabric the next month. And by the time my mom starts to follow her latest vegan recipes, she has already moved on to hosting a travel show, talking about biking and backpacking.

I am the specimen for administrating all the above opinions. Out of fear, respect and helplessness, I am the scapegoat for trying out all the knowledge that my magnetic mom musters every day.

Adults are suckers for information. They like it even if it is incorrect. They prefer 'wrong' information to 'no' information, says Rolf Dobelli in *The Art of Thinking Clearly*. Also, more information falsely increases their confidence and it is very easy to lose their common sense amidst so much information that is received all day long.

Our parents love information, maybe because it was very hard to get when they were children. Since they had to rummage through books or felt stranded due to lack of information in their childhood, they are very eager to lap it all up now. They want us also to know everything about everything while we are just not keen on filling our heads with information. It is so readily available now that it is not as valuable as our parents think.

A plant needs moisture, not water for growth. When more water is given, it leads to leaching of nutrition. Also, plants become succulent and hence, vulnerable to pests. Please give us moisture, not overdose of water.

We are happy communicating in short forms and emojis while you need so many words. Just text me the next time you wish to say something to me. I will surely reply with a 'thumbs-up' emoji.

How about a talking and typing detox to tackle us better?

REASON 18

The P4: Permanent Persuasive Power of Parents

I always see my father jiggle the lock after securing the door. It is amusing to see a self-assured man always in doubt about his door-locking skills. Often, he comes back from the car to double-check the door, which must be writhing in pain due to his heavy shaking of the knob.

It all fell in place the day I observed my grandfather doing the same while locking the heavy doors of our home in Rajasthan. He rotated the keys inside the lock, checked the handle, pushed the door back and forth and then came out. He sat in the car and asked me, 'Just go and check whether the door is locked properly'. I rolled my eyes in disbelief and was about to open my mouth in protest but my grandmother indicated to me to go and push the poor door once more.

My dad subconsciously does what my grandfather does.

Parents wield their power over children through genes. Parents wield some more power by passing on some habits to their children. Their power becomes too much when our beliefs and opinions become Mummy-fied and Daddy-fied.

We come in this world with a gift of their genes. The gift is wrapped by their habits with a ribbon of their beliefs tucked on it.

I watch a film and my first reaction is, 'I like it', unless I hear my mom tearing it apart. I read an autobiography of a national hero and start to admire his life journey. Suddenly, I hear my dad talking about him as a marketing mastermind. His thoughts start rankling me.

Their general opinions, like 'People of X community are good', 'Never trust any person from Y state', 'Dark skin tone is not beautiful', become a part of our 'growing-up narrative' and then we get irrationally attached to theses generalizations. Why do you share your opinions with us? Damn it, they impact us. We start thinking like you. Your judgemental attitude, your biases seep into us. And God forbid, when we don't agree with you, you hate us.

Your judgemental mindset and opinionated behaviour influences our growing-up years because:

- ◆ You want us to behave in accordance to your opinions. You neither expect us to like a person you dislike nor allow us to do so. A respondent mentioned that her father got upset when she spoke to one of his cousin's daughter for a long time at a function, because he did not like that cousin of his.
- ◆ You stick to your opinions and beliefs. A friend of mine was given detention in school for bullying a younger child. It has been two years and though he improved and never misbehaved again, you firmly guarded your opinion about him. Your mindset is overpowering and fixed wherever your children are concerned.
- ◆ You only like 'like-minded people'. We want to be liked by you. So we let ourselves become your cover version. I recently met a 6-year-old girl who was excessively chirpy around her mom and me. She sang loudly, pulled my hair and performed some somersaults. As

soon as her father came, she became another person. Her tone changed while talking to him,

'How was your day, Daddy?'

'Good. How was yours?'

'Oh! It was nice. I loved school. I came and took a nap.'

'What did you eat?'

'I had milk shake.'

'Homework?'

'Finished.'

'Good.'

'Good night everyone. Good night, Dad.'

She walked back to her room quietly.

I felt like I was watching the little girl in a double role in a Hindi film. So much for getting liked.

Do you want to know about the power wielded by parents over their children and, hence, the world? Had it not been for parents of Robert Clive, India would not have been ruled by Britain for so long. Robert was a fearless and unruly child. As his poor parents could neither educate him nor nurture him, he became quite a handful.

Robert's father, assuming a bleak future for his son, got him employed as a clerk in the East India Company. At 18, he was sent to Madras (now Chennai). He took military training and consolidated the British Army against the French Empire. His disapproving father changed the future of our country. Clive never wanted to come to India but he had to bow down to his father's wishes. The founder of the British Empire in our country dominated mercilessly over everyone but got dominated by his father.[35] This is the kind of power you exercise over us.

PV Sindhu, the famous Indian shuttler recently admitted on a TV show that her father, an Arjuna awardee and a famous volley ball player, encouraged her to be a sportsperson, but not in a team sport. That is why she chose badminton where she could be the only recipient of all the glory. This is the kind of power you exercise over us.

I tried to please you and seek your approval in the first decade of my life but the next decade brought out a rebel in me. Your mission to control me is met with my mission to resist you with all my might.

The more you push me, the more I push back. The more you threaten me, the more I talk back.

A father shows his authority when he says, 'I am your father, you are not my father.' A mother uses her emotional power when she says, 'I am your mother, and this is how you talk to me?'

My dopamine levels are soaring right now. I argue with you, challenge you and defy you because you are the safest point for me to vent out, to mess up.

This is my first childhood, but for you, it is the second. You saw yours too. Please don't deny your run-ins with your parents when you were young. You will always influence our mindsets, our opinions and our habits because we are cut from the same cloth.

---

[35]https://www.theguardian.com/world/2015/mar/04/east-india-company-original-corporate-raiders

I do not wish to push you down when I disagree with you, I want to pull myself up.

I do not intend to ignore you, when I defy you, I want to seek myself out.

Please be patient when I shout, throw my hands or things and howl helplessly.

Whenever I run a race, I run faster in the last few seconds because I know that I can use all the buried energy just before the end. When you guys can see our adulthood round the corner, please muster all the buried patience to deal with our power struggles.

You are my 'stage' to play out my emotions.

I do not want to suppress it because I do not wish to poison myself in the long run.

Be the stage beneath my shaky feet and absorb my tears. If you hit back, I will topple.

How about replacing 'anger' with 'patience' from your default setting?

After all, you are my father. I am not yours.

REASON 19

Been There, Done That

A respondent of my survey shared that she wished to join a hotel management course after high school. To help her, the mother googled 'Top Colleges for Hotel Management'. She also searched websites for best culinary courses. In the next few days, her feed started receiving ads of various such courses. Her inbox soon started getting promotional mails from the admission offices of several hotel management colleges. She inferred that these courses are 'in demand'. Unaware about 'cookies', she fell for the 'confirmation bias' smoothly.[36]

I cannot forget one of the many hilarious beliefs my grandmother has: 'Whenever you go on stage, put your left foot first and hold on for a millisecond before you go further.'

I won a debate competition after her instruction and she told me happily, 'See, the method works!' She doesn't know that I never did it. Who would remember to put the left foot forward when stage fright is killing every atom in my wobbly brain?

New parents, being clueless about the dos and don'ts, frenetically look for advice through various mediums, such as books, the Internet, experienced mothers and even their own experiences.

They begin at the wide bottom of the pyramid, paying

---

[36]Confirmation bias is the tendency to interpret new evidence as confirmation of one's existing beliefs or theories.

focused attention to all and sundry. The more attention they give, the more confused they become. One parenting expert vehemently advocates an infant to sleep with the parents in their bed, another expert propagates a separate bed for newborns to make them independent and comfortable.

One experienced mom vouches for baby food and diapers, while for a grandmother, they are a strict no-no. One online platform advises mothers to stay at home for the first thousand days, while the other cites research which doesn't find it of much consequence.

Parents pick some advice, drop some after use and sieve through the expert clutter till they find that one expert of their choice—themselves.

Once they sit on the top of the pyramid of experts, they start giving 'gyan' to other clueless parents who have just begun at the bottom of the pyramid.

Each parent tunes out everything contrary to their expert advice and collects supporting evidence for their advice. They get enough proof to prove whatever they believe in.

Parents who believe 'Friends are harbingers of doom' have enough stories stored on the tip of their tongues to prove how these friends pressurize other children to bully, get involved into substance abuse and disturb study plans.

Similarly, parents who ardently believe in 'Friends are happiness personified' know children who help, collaborate, motivate, share and care at every step.

The former set of parents avoids the heart-warming stories of friendship, declaring them imaginary; while the latter ignores the negative influences of friendship by saying that 'friends for benefits' are not real friends.

Parents preserve their political and religious beliefs and

expect children to follow the same. A father who supports the current government will forward daily messages applauding its schemes and speeches. A vegetarian family mines for data to prove that a majority of the world population is turning vegetarian, which is the moral way of life; while non-vegetarians ask, 'How can people survive on a vegetarian diet?' However, plenty of twin and adoption research studies conducted in the US and Europe prove that parenting influences the political label accepted by children but not their political attitudes and beliefs. Ditto for religion.[37]

Parents walk in our lives with their cups overflowing. They keep adding to it from all possible sources. How about walking in dumb for some time at least? How about letting go of all biases, prejudices and gained knowledge and face yourself without being insecure about not knowing much?

How about alighting down from the pedestal of being an expert to just being alive—open to new ideas full of wonder and possibility?

There is a critic and creator hidden in all of us. Knowledge stokes the fire in the critic's belly while curiosity ignites the creator's heart. We need a creator more who works with us on the easel and less of a critic who sits on the armchair and judges our work at the easel.

A child undergoes major transition every three to four years

---

[37]Bryan Caplan. 'The Parental Wishlist, wish #6'. In: *Selfish Reasons to Have More Kids: Why being a great parent is less work and more fun than you think.* 2012. New York: Basic Books.

till his/her adulthood.[38] *A parent, being the coach, needs to be ahead of the transition curve. To stay ahead, parents have no time to say: 'I have figured it out now'. They need to raise their game to be in a position of silent observers who strategize with agility and at every phase.*

Strategies that worked in terrible twos will not see you through tween tantrums.

Since I am not a product that comes with a user manual, how about mentally orchestrating your moves to help me be who I can?

Since I am a unique creation of you two, how about answering all the tough questions related to me by looking for answers inside you or me?

The fragrance haunting a musk deer lies inside him only while he keeps running in all directions in its search!

---

[38]Swati Lodha. 2016. *Don't Raise Your Children, Raise Yourself.* New Delhi: StoryMirror Infotech. p. 78.

REASON 20

The Punishment Paradox

I get a lot of anecdotal evidence around punishment meted out by Indian parents. Our parents' generation talks about physical punishment as a regular feature of its childhood. Apparently, meting out physical punishment made a parent eligible for being lauded as competent.

Times have changed now. Modes of punishment have altered. Yelling has become a unit of communication. Punishment is less predictable now. With stress going up and patience going down, any small wrong can evoke a harsh punishment from parents.

How does punishment originate in our family lives? It arises from a parent's basic thought: 'You'd better think like me and do as I say. If you don't, I will make you have some negative experiences you won't like.'

You evoke fear in us. Are you sure that you want us to be scared of you?

In the process, you end up evoking hatred in us. Just as trees, after pruning, shed countless branches, we emit a lot of hatred after receiving punishment.

Let me give away the spoiler: Your ways of punishment make your children fearful and angry. They are not reforming or improving us.

We all have faced some form of punishment in our lives—a 'time out', 'getting hit', 'being ignored', 'being humiliated' or 'being subjected to mean behaviour'. You guys punish us in plenty. You do so because:

- You suffer from this insurmountable fear that I will turn into this ill-behaved, rude slob if you would not correct me constantly. You worry about my future.
- You grew up believing that 'not agreeing' with you is a reason enough to invite punishment from you. I break a glass and I get yelled at. I yell and I get 'time out'. I do not respond out of anger and you tune me out for hours, may be days.
- You want to succeed at your parenting job. You would be termed careless and irresponsible if I do not turn out to be a 'perfect' child who is an academic genius, a social wonder, a champion in arts and sports with a million online followers on at least Instagram.

Parents love to give 'unrelated punishments'. They say things like,

'If you forget to call me when you reach your friend's place, I will confiscate your phone for a day.'

'If you physically harm your younger brother, you cannot watch TV for a week.'

Next time even if I remember to call you after reaching my friend's place, I am doing it because I do not want to lose my phone for a day and not because I feel responsible.

Also, half of the punishment gets diluted. Who will remember to check 'No TV' rule for a week? You lose credibility as a disciplinarian the moment your execution falters. Do you only want a 'buy-in' for now, not a responsible child for future?

When you punish 'there and then', ask yourself: Are you merely venting your anger or working towards making us better?

When I defy you, you slap me. This is retributive justice—blood for blood. Am I a primitive criminal?

When I defy you, you confiscate my phone. This is deterrence—a warning. Am I a terrorist?[39]

My cousin told me that once he got beaten up with a leather belt when he did not tell his test marks to his parents and forged their signatures.

What happened to a friend in a similar situation was the most hilarious (Although, what he did was still wrong.): When he was caught by his teacher for forging his mother's signature, the mother was summoned to school. The principal suggested to her, 'Congratulations madam! Your son can replace you now. So, he will cook for himself, iron his clothes himself and will pay his bus fee, too, on his own.'

The principal told my friend, 'Since you signed for your mother, you think you can replace her. I respect your thought.'

The friend apologized in all possible ways and was consequently forgiven.

Noted economist Bryan Caplan says that whenever he puts his kids in the 'naughty corner', they apologize for their offences and their behaviour improves for a short period, before going back to their old tricks. This makes him wonder: 'If I can't change what my sons are going to do next month, how can I hope to change what they're going to do when they're adults.'

Hope you guys are listening to Caplan!

I got slapped for the first time when I was 5 years old. One day, I had suddenly asked my mother, 'Who is my stepmom?

---

[39]There are five theories of Punishment: Retributive, Deterrent, Preventive, Reformative and Expiatory.

Where is she? I want to meet her. Thanks to Cinderella and her *'Oh-so realistic tale',* I thought everyone had a stepmother. Since then, my mother has regretted that slap on many occasions (I ensured that she does), though it was utterly ridiculous. Was my curiosity worth that slap (which still rings in my ears every time I see Cinderella running back from the Ball)?

Just ask yourself, would you like to be hit, yelled at or insulted? If I become abusive and rude towards you and justify it by saying, 'I didn't mean it. I was just tired/hormonal', would you forgive and forget?

How you punish and why you punish are as important as the act of punishing itself.[40]

I yell, argue and slam doors and laptops. Bear with me, reach out to me. Make it clear that I need to find better ways to express myself.

If you start competing with me in yelling and name-calling, followed by a sob session, I will never learn how to act responsibly.

Some parents say that they feel helpless and hence resort to punishment, while some say that their ego gets hurt and hence they punish. If you punish due to these reasons, the parent in you is getting punished, not me.

The next time I forget to text you after reaching somewhere, do not say anything then. When I wish to go somewhere the next time, tell me with a smile that I can't go because I suffer from forgetfulness. This is called 'consequence', not 'punishment'.

---

[40] Malcolm Gladwell says so in *David & Goliath*, p. 208.

REASON 21

Operate. Manipulate. Negotiate.

I am a sucker for grocery stores. I love the vibe, the colourful rows of stacked snacks, the moving trolleys with mommies on mission and the curious toddlers on their own journey. These are also hotspots for interesting observations. Very often, I notice some little boy trying all his tactics—vocal, spatial, theatrical—to push a particular purchase out of his mom. After a matching theatrical performance by the mom, the negotiation begins.

'OK, Mumma will buy this, but you will have to be a good boy for the whole week.'

The child immediately turns docile and disciplined, while the harried mother seems relieved and triumphant.

Consider another scenario: A child flunks a particular subject test, say Maths. Parents are worried. They throw bait, 'You ace your test and we buy you a phone.'

It is so common to focus fully on tackling a test set for tomorrow that, somehow, we miss preparing for the bigger exam.

A win-win situation indeed. It is commonly used by parents because it works.

When a child sprawls on the grocery store's floor, hollering for a bottle of soda, and gets it, the manipulator wins. The mother and son do not. When the son aces Maths test to get the new phone, the negotiator wins. The father and son do not.

Parents allow, rather facilitate, our transition from being children to deal brokers.

You guys negotiate with us because:

- **We give you a hard time and you do not have time.** When I walk disinterestedly towards the finishing line of 'Maths', you dangle a phone and I run to win the race. I feel like a dog now. You change my behaviour by showing stimuli.

    You are offering us fish but not teaching us how to fish. You keep us dependent on you. My mother showed me this amazing post on a social media group—'Tell us how you emotionally blackmail your children'. There were 132 comments by smart mothers. A couple of gems were:

    'If you misbehave, I will take "work from home" option from office.'

    'If you do not listen to me, I will leave you alone.'

    Should I behave well so that I don't have to survive 'you' the whole day? Should I listen to you only because I need you?

    You ignite our 'extrinsic motivation', while extinguishing any amber of intrinsic motivation gleaming in any corner of our being.

- **You are 'fixing' us up like a small irritating part in your life's machine, so that it keeps functioning today.** The glitch is that this small irritating part is neither replaceable nor rectifiable at a later date.

    You give us wrong ideas: 'Finish the veggies and you get the ice cream.' 'If you finish the prescribed course of your exam, you can see the soccer game.'

> An ice cream reward sends a subtle signal that veggies are not worth eating on their own. You are giving me the wrong idea that I should love and enjoy ice cream more than the veggies.
>
> The soccer game reward signals that finishing the portion requires a reward. If studying systematically would be a good choice, why would you need to reward me with a soccer game? You are giving me the wrong idea that studying systematically is not as good as a soccer game.[41]

You pay us with an ice cream to eat veggies. You pay us with a soccer game to finish the scheduled study. When you stop paying, I stop eating or studying at a fast pace.

If you incentivize our behaviour, it focuses on result and not the intent. Such behaviour is not long-lasting. Such behaviour doesn't stand out on its own.

Also, when you don't eat vegetables, why would we want to do so? If broccoli is first thing on your plate, I will mimic you easily.[42]

We all must have had this experience, at least once in our lives. When you leave food on your plate, you are told, 'Don't waste food. You are fortunate to get it. Millions of children are not that fortunate and go hungry.' Many mothers and grandmothers have shoved morsels up our throats to teach us to value food. I understand that we must not waste food. We should also recognize that there are many children who

---

[41] Jonah Berger. 2015. *Invisible Influence: The Hidden Forces That Shape Behavior*. New York: Simon & Schuster. p. 62.

[42] Operant Conditioning by B.F. Skinner; https://www.learning-theories.com/operant-conditioning-skinner.html

go without a square meal a day.

But how would the leftover in my plate help the needy? Either we have a mechanism to share leftovers with the needy immediately or it gets stored in our refrigerator to be finally trashed.

The lesson to fill the plate or glass only as much as one can finish is perfectly fine. But pushing us to overeat has nothing to do with others going hungry.

For the last few days, my mom would come to my room every night and casually hand over whatever she had written that day.

'You rate whatever I have written. Out of 7.' I obey her.

'You get a 4.5 on this one.'

'Ok. I will work harder. I want to get at least a 6.'

Next day, she hands me her work again.

'Read and rate this. Out of seven please!' I oblige again.

'Oh, it is a 5 today.'

I gave proper feedback on sentence formation, imagery, clarity. She nodded.

'I want it to be a 6, at least.'

Well, she returns the next day.

'This is actually nice. A 5.5 today.'

'Good. I am improving. I can aim for a 7 now!'

'Relax Mom!'

She smiled and left.

This seemed mysterious. I needed to know what this woman was up to. So the next day, as soon as I returned home from school, I asked her, 'What did you write today?'

'Nothing. I need more focus. I need to cut some noise, please keep my phone in your room today so that I can write in peace.'

'What? You want me to get disturbed.'

'Oh! Sorry. Fine, I will keep it in the living room.'
She did what she said.
She didn't show me anything for two days. Then, she showed up.
'See this now. Rate it please. Out of...'
'Out of 7, I know.'
What she wrote was really impressive. It was an article on digital discipline.
'This is 6 plus.'
'The next step is a 7.' She responded with a high five.
And then it struck me.
I am a student of the International Baccalaureate (IB) programme where we are marked out of 7 in every subject. To be sure of her intentions, I sneaked into her Kindle and there it was.

She was reading, *Nudge: Improving decisions about health, wealth and happiness.*[43]

What an amazing way to 'nudge' me to think only about number 7.

Negotiating to condition us to behave in a particular way is akin to treating us like pets.

Please make us accountable by being responsible yourself. Nudge us in the right direction to decide, rather than crack a deal with us.

How about 'exemplifying' rather than 'explaining'?
How about changing 'If you...I will...' to 'I do...because...'?

---

[43]Richard H. Thaler and Cass R. Sunstein. 2012. *Nudge: Improving decisions about health, wealth and happiness.* New York: Penguin.

REASON 22

Cryptic Cure of 'Cozy Consensus'

Famous psychologist Solomon Asch conducted an experiment in the 1950s: A subject is shown a paper which has a line drawn on it; three other lines, numbered 1, 2 and 3, are drawn next to it—one shorter, one longer and one similar in length to the original one. He is asked to tell which one of the three matched in length with the original line. In each trial, when he responds on his own, he mostly gives the correct answer. Then, five people, all actors (which the subject is unaware of), enter the room and all give wrong answers. When the subject is asked again, one-third of the times, he answers incorrectly in order to match his answer with the other respondents.

The result of the experiment: Adults change their behaviour in groups.

Parents also fall in the trap of 'group thinking' because:

- **It is scary to be a lonely parent.** Since you are always new at what you are doing as a parent (each child is a unique minefield, you see!), it is comforting to have some more parents in your decision-making process. You don't feel alone even if the action is purely foolish. Collective foolishness is a cushion against the anxiety-laden wait to witness the results of our foolish actions. Since it is painful to be a lone warrior, we all seek allies. Parents have their allies in people who have children (friends of my parents) or who deal with children (my teachers). Such allies influence them at home, at workplace, at kitty parties, at school meetings, in WhatsApp groups and during interaction on social networking sites. As parents, you feel lonely, stressed and insecure, and so there is a natural urge to open up to someone. Groups of parents who share the same kinds of insecurities and stress feel safe and sane together. When they start copying the actions of each other, it becomes dangerous.

- **Groups give pseudo trust.** When everyone is doing it, it must be good. If so many people are going to these classes, they must be giving good results. If so many people are watching these videos, they must be good. *'Hema, Rekha, Jaya aur Sushma… Sabki pasand Nirma'* is *'Cozy Consensus'* at its best.

  Parents bask in the glory of *social validation*. When Disney launched Baby Einstein videos, young mothers considered them to be a great tool to teach young children. The videos are useless for toddlers as all they do is make them addicted to the computer screens, but they are useful for mothers in satisfying their real desire of social validation by other moms.

- **Groups offer collective confidence.** More than right or wrong, parents love to agree and be agreed by others. If four friends are buying tetra packs of milk, the fifth one will pick the habit without using her brains. Their decisions bask in the warmth of similar minds. It makes them confident when they have others with them. Togetherness grants a pseudo confidence, just like in a mob. In a group, an authority figure mentions a few things which others begin to obey. Later, even when the authority figure moves on or turns his back on the idea, the glue of cohesion keeps the group together. We love to hang with some people even with the insanely thin threads of lingering togetherness.

- **Nothing draws a crowd like a crowd.** Now, this is very specific to our country. Indians believe in cult following, which makes them inclined towards joining mom groups or parenting forums. We are always eager to surrender our logical mind at the altar of collective stupidity.

Frequently, families resemble cliques, where each family member is forced or conditioned to act in a certain way. Seven physicians, five gynaecologists, three ophthalmologists, three ENT specialists with some surgeons, pathologists and paediatricians make two generations of a family I know in Jaipur.[44]

An advocate dad had eight children and seven of them became doctors and the next generation took the bend forward. It is possible that the seniors encouraged the younger siblings. It is possible that the elder ones found some key methods to crack the medical entrance exam. The youngest child of the family, the best basketball player of her state team, chose medicine over basketball as it had become a family tradition.

That is how families, the first unit of a group, function. Siblings follow each other because their family environment and regular conversations feature similar themes. 'Medicine' becomes the comfort zone

---

[44]www.timesofindia.indiatimes.com/city/Jaipur/31-doctors-in-this-jaipur-family-still-countingarticleshow/37068783.cms

for families full of doctors. It becomes a problem for those children who wish to break the family tradition.

- **Group thinking causes knowledge illusion.** When everyone follows everyone and keeps the information and analysis to themselves, the value of group is lost. When parents fall in the trap of 'group thinking', no one wants to spoil the party. Everyone tends to sing along even when some of them know that they are singing to boredom. Emotions run high among such groups and no one dares to be the devil's advocate. We suffer from a 'knowledge illusion',[45] thinking that we know a lot. The reality is that we know very little individually but consider knowledge in the minds of others as our own.

Jonah Berger, in his book, *Invisible Influence: The Hidden Forces That Shape Behavior*,[46] talks about a parking lot at a country fair without any white lines and, of course, no attendant. When the first car enters the lot, the driver parks it facing west as he prefers it that way. When the next person comes in, though he prefers parking his car facing east, he ends up parking west, just like the previous car. Anyone who comes in later, parks facing west only.

Imagine what would have happened had the second man entered before the first and parked his car facing east? It would have led everyone to keep their cars in the parking lot, facing east. The parking lot would have looked absolutely different.

---

[45] https://www.nytimes.com/2017/04/18/books/review/knowledge-illusion-steven-sloman-philip-fernbach.html
[46] Berger, *Invisible Influence*.

When J.K. Rowling writes *The Cuckoo's Calling* under a pseudonym Robert Galbraith, it merely sells 1,500 hardcover copies in three months. Later, as soon as the real identity of the author is revealed, it becomes a bestselling book, moving from a 4,709th rank on Amazon.

If it is J.K. Rowling, it has to be a bestseller.

Parents love to believe in these social influences. That is why we end up eating 'healthy' biscuits endorsed by babas and bowing in front of them in crowded ashrams.

Another example can be of WhatsApp group chats. If one person wishes 'Happy Birthday' to a friend on a Whatsapp group, your phone will be flooded with similar message by all friends in the next half an hour. It is disturbing, irritating but not harmful. But when parents use thoughts, behaviours and actions of others to form their own thoughts, behaviours and actions, it can disfigure the lives of their children.

Choosing a school just because all your friends are clamouring to get their kids admitted to that school, selecting a sport because every parent around is doing so is akin to jumping in the well on seeing your neighbour do so. And when he comes out with his house keys that had accidentally fallen into the well, you start looking for an answer to his 'Why did "You" jump into the well?'

'Herd Moms' send their children to study centres to prepare for prestigious exams because everyone else is doing it. 'Herd Dads' take bank loans to send the children abroad for higher studies, because they notice other people talk with grandiosity about their children studying in a community college in Honolulu!

Though our lineage inspires us to copy, can we restrict it to areas which do not have a long-lasting impact on us? 'When in Rome, do as the Romans do—which means eat like them or make merry like them. But don't let your stereotypical image of Rome ruin our present.

How about not being a part of such groups? If you don't observe such people, they do not influence you. If you are not part of such Whatsapp groups, we are safe. When you stand in queues waiting to enter a popular restaurant, we all fall in the trap of assuming that we are eating at the best place. It is only a fervent recommendation which grows exponentially due to groupthink. There could probably be equally good places which would make our weekend enjoyable.

We observe you when you run to be a part of group; we learn that it is better to follow others than oneself. When you create your life anchors outside, we learn the same.

Then comes the twist. You chose my school as your colleague's kids go to the same school. When I want to go for a trip because all my friends are going, you use your emotional powers to dissuade me from taking that trip. You love your allies and listen to them. You dislike my confidants and disapprove completely when I listen to them. You listen more to your friends than your parents. When we do the same, we are labelled impractical and defiant.

Rather than making a group with other parents and friends, how about making a group with us? Though it will take you out of like-mindedness and self-confirming newsfeeds, it will be a welcome change and challenge.

REASON 23

More People, Less Responsibility

It was a group project at school. Some of the group members did not show any interest in working on it. I realized that I had been paired with a bunch of laggards and I needed to carry the project on my Hermione-turned-Hulk shoulders.

Whenever my parents come to know about such predicaments, they jump on their beloved conclusions:

'X is not doing anything because he knows that you will finish it come what may.'

'Y is finding faults in what you are doing and not adding anything else. I am telling you, he is jealous.'

'Z will still get his grades, even if he doesn't show up. This is cool. You work and others enjoy. They are taking advantage of you.'

Whenever we are working on a group project, we have certain ups and downs of happiness and horror.

Whatever the situation, we go through our share of heartburn and hope. You, as parents, do not like to see us going through the pressure, pain and panic caused by other children.

You ask us, 'Why are you taking all the burden?' 'Why are others using you to get everything done?' 'You are an easy prey.'

You do not want us to give our 100 per cent effort in a collective project. According to you, when the responsibility is on many shoulders, then individual responsibility gets reduced. If nobody is doing anything, I should follow suit. Everyone feels that someone else would do it.

On my first day in my new school, I was unable to follow the accent of my Scottish teacher who was teaching us Principles of Business. When I looked around, everyone had a Ron Weasley (read confused) look on their faces, yet no one spoke up. Being new, I kept quiet, and waited for someone else to speak up.

When my mother came to know about my silence, she didn't like it. She expected me to take responsibility. But, when I wanted to take responsibility earlier in a group by finishing the given tasks, she wanted me to diffuse it.

Not only this, my mother said, 'Had I been you, I would have surely spoken up. If you do not understand something, speak up. To hell with the others!'

Professor Max Bazerman calls this 'behavioural forecasting error'. How we think we would behave is pretty different from how we actually behave. Parents think ideally, but behave humanly. When you guys talk to us, your 'should self' does the talking. This 'should self' is the perfect self who does the right thing.[47]

When you guys really go out there and act, your 'want self' does the doing. This 'want self' is your real self who does what it feels right at that moment. Parents mess up in sending the right and righteous signals to us because they love us too much.

You try to correct our actions all the time because your individual attitude differs from your social norms.

You teach us idealistically as an individual to help others in need. But when you witness an accident on the road with crowd around it, you do not go out and help. You assume that

---

[47] Bezerman and Tenbrunsel, *Blind Spots,* p. 66.

someone in the crowd would surely do it, if needed.

When I suffer from pluralistic ignorance, you disapprove. But then, you suffer from it all the time.[48]

A student who graduated from a top Indian college, shared, 'Drinking alcohol is a social norm at college. Though I see my friends suffering from vomiting and headaches and though I realize its negative impact on my academic performance, these realizations affect my private attitude, not the social norm. We continue to consume alcohol in groups.'[49]

Behaviour of parents becomes annoying because:

- They let their social norms overpower their individual attitudes. Their individuality turns into slush in a group.
- They do not expect us to fall prey to pluralistic ignorance based on their evaluation of the situation. However, they suffer from it all the time.

Your 'should-self' is idealistic and preaches us to be bold. Your 'want-self' is realistic and tells us to 'take it easy' in a group. How about allowing me to pivot my thoughts and behaviours as per my analysis of the situation?

How about pressing 'later' on the warning bell in your head? We need to admit that it is essential to reduce the gap between our individual beliefs and social norms.

Adults in mobs and crowds behave more violently and irresponsibly as they feel anonymous in a group. Digital trolling

---

[48] Pluralistic ignorance occurs when people erroneously infer that they feel differently from their peers, even though they are behaving similarly; http://changingminds.org/explanations/theories/pluralistic_ignorance.htm

[49] He shared it easily as he had been my mother's student.

is a kind of faceless mob behaviour that causes animosity, negativity and hurt for everyone. Even when no one knows, I know what I did. This cannot be explained, it can only be shown.

If you get 'deindividuated' in a group, we will follow you quickly to learn that faceless mobs are the safe havens. If you mask yourself to vent out, I will learn that 'ambush and attack' works everywhere, not only in war zones. If you dilute your identity in a group by diffusing your responsibility, I will learn to have two faces—a sophisticated, 'I' face and a crude 'group' face—with confidence.

How about showing us to keep our real and unambiguous face on, 24x7? Guess what? It will keep me away from peer pressure and social contagion.

Who knows it better than me, who has two people in her life who wear their 'authenticity' on their sleeves. My dad is a poet and stand-up comic, which means that authenticity is his occupation.

My mom is perhaps cognitively challenged to notice 'groups'. She shows me every day 'how to drop unproductive battles and focus on relevant ones'.

I have peers but 'no pressure'. 'I' work with groups. I am neither 'popular' in school nor have a long friends list on social media.

But, I love myself.

REASON 24

Peaks and Ends

I went for my friend's sixteenth birthday bash. Music, masti, loads of fun. The venue was known to my mom (well, she dropped me!). She had told me to get free by 11.00 p.m. And, as usual, she reached to pick me fifteen minutes earlier and called me fifteen times in those fifteen minutes.

Since a few of us friends had planned to leave together, we came out at five minutes past eleven.

There she was—her panic mode in full throttle. Her face was a kaleidoscope of fear, anger, frustration, anxiety that sucked up all my 'fun time' in a flash.

'What happened?' I asked.

'Look at your phone.' She stressed at every word as if double clicking each one.

I whispered a meek bye to all my friends to escape further embarrassment.

Before I could say anything, she began to shout about how tense she grew with each missed call.

She called me irresponsible, selfish, careless and many other names that I don't remember. But I do remember how I felt.

A beautiful evening that ended on such a sad note.

Parents are masterpieces who have a special knack for making things end badly. When my class teacher praises me profusely in front of her, my mother smiles with pride.

Later, she cuts me to size. 'No need to be so happy. She says this to each parent.' Ouch!

I attempted eighteen mock tests while preparing for my ACT exam. It was a preparation of around hundred hours. I was happy with my performance which steadily improved with each test.

And then she wiped off all the prep with one verbal sweep: 'I am worried about the final exam. You didn't score well the last time.'

It doesn't occur to her anxiety-laden mind that I didn't prepare enough last time. All my confidence crumbled with her icy words.

My friend shared her observation: Every family vacation begins with excitement and ends in sadness for parents and trauma for us. Visiting each museum, each park and each tower is so boring and then you have to fake happiness all the time. As soon as your excitement dips at these weary tourist spots, you will be called inconsiderate and ungrateful.

'We have spent so much, we have planned it all to make you happy. But, nothing is good enough for you,' shouts one of the parents.

Truth be told, most family vacations are actually opposite of enjoyment and fun.

Parents, at the end, just remember it as an expensive exercise which they took to give a lifetime of experiences to their children. While children generally end up synthesizing a painful memory. High control and expectations kill the vacation vibe and create a sad memory for us.

Our memories of those experiences are very different. Our memory scores each experience as good, bad or worse at two junctures:

- Peaks, i.e. the worst or the best moments during their experience.

- Ends, i.e. the good or the bad feeling at the end.[50]

Parents are so focused on making our 'future adulthood' that they embark on a journey breaking our 'present childhood'.

Our happy memories of childhood are moments of sheer joy spent with people we love.

When I asked many of my friends to share such happy memories of their childhood with their parents, most of them shared many happy toddler memories, some tween memories and finally a fade-out.

There are fewer experiences that end well as we grow into double-digit years. You guys bicker, belittle, criticize and disapprove most of what we do during high school and college years. It gives us negative experiences for present and unhappy memories for future.

When we reach adulthood, our whole journey of childhood becomes 'one experience' for you guys. If I turn out fine according to your standards, I get placed in your minds as a reasonably happy memory. All the mutual heartburn and brain bashing disappears. For us, each experience is a separate chunk of our life with its peak and ends throbbing in our hearts. We have a long trail of good, bad and worse memories which you would not even recognize.

Each one of us measures our life experiences in terms of pleasure and pain. Our 'experiencing self' experiences it once and has no voice later while our 'remembering self' is active throughout our lives.

That is how our remembering selves are as different as a

---

[50] https://www.behavioraleconomics.com/mini-encyclopedia-of-be/peak-end-rule/

pizza and a pen drive and our memories of our same experience pan out so differently.

I had a major fallout with a close friend an year ago. Though the end was really painful, we had amazing memories of our friendship. For my parents, the bad end made it all bad. They remember her as a blotch in my childhood while my 'remembering self' has a different picture printed due to many happy peaks involved.

Because of our parents' attachment with the end experience, they love our pay packages so much. You guys love to talk about them as the last leg of all the hard work done by you during our school and college years.

Parents fail to empathize with us as their versions of our childhood are very different from ours. Our 'remembering selves' create stories as different as chalk and cheese for future use. We still know about their versions as they keep repeating them, especially if we caused them heartache but they do not know about ours as we do not have the guts to tell them how they made us feel.

We are an overjet family, meaning all three of us have protruding front teeth. Though my dad got it treated when he was a child and I have been going through the process for the last five years, my mom is still a monument of outwardly inclined front teeth. My grandmother refused to get her teeth treated when she was a child and my mother obeyed her decision which she has grown to loathe more with every spoilt photograph of hers.

For my grandmother, it is a 'small happy memory' of a conscious mother who preserved four healthy teeth of her daughter and did not succumb to social expectations of 'the face matters most for a girl'.

Peaks and Ends

For my mom, it is an ongoing experience of regret for not correcting an easily correctable flaw at a young age.

What ended pretty positively for my grandmom peaks pretty painfully for my mom even now.

'Half a century from now, your children will remember how you treated them. If you showed them kindness they probably won't forget. If you habitually lost your temper, they probably won't forget that either. Out of all the wishes on the Parental Wish List, "good memories" are one of the few that clearly depend upon how you raise your child. Don't forget it,' says my favourite parent, Bryan Caplan.[51]

Since we all remember peaks and ends of our experiences more and since we all have different peaks and ends of the same experiences, we should communicate our remembrances to each other.

Parents should respect the 'felt memories' of a child when he tells them about how miserable they made him feel in that particular moment.

Rather than trying to justify their behaviour, they should positively accept the feelings that got formed in the child while they were not aware about it at all.

A Parent–Child relationship doesn't end with the child reaching adulthood, it gets transformed. How about being transparent in sharing your mutual feelings (if you have not done so before) in future? It might help younger siblings or at least repair your existing relationship.

---

[51] Caplan, *Selfish Reasons,* Chapter 2.

REASON 25

The Perfect Child Syndrome

What gives you the great idea that we can excel in all areas—academics, sports, arts, social skills, creativity.

Every parent loves an Einstein brain, though none understands the theory of relativity.

Each parent has one common dream which they see as a fundamental right—Our child should be perceived as perfect by everyone. They turn from a grain of rice to puffed rice by the mere thought of their child being appreciated by all.

He should be an ideal child to his teachers, the helping friend to his classmates, the most suitable boy to the girls, the smiling guy to the maids and drivers and the prodigal son to the parents. In short, he needs to play to the gallery. He needs to be the nicest guy 24x7.

I become a chameleon who tirelessly tries to make everyone happy without thinking about what brings me happiness. Parents design perfect happiness for me, which is perceived as perfect.

Why didn't you tell me that you didn't want a child but a chameleon who would change her personality with every social encounter?

Just as innovators have a tendency to embed too many features in their initial product design, you wish to embed too many activities in our lives. Just as new authors are deeply inclined to use complex words and puzzling theories, you are keen on having your children get involved into as many activities as possible, that too, the more complex sounding they are, the better it is.

'My son enjoys paragliding and kayaking. Oh, he went for barefoot skiing and it was an experience of a lifetime.'

'My daughter is looking at a degree in "symbolic systems"[52] with special interest in Captology.'[53]

On hearing such statements, the parent listening and his child will drown deep in depression. He would go home and take refuge under the wings of Google. The child would feel inferior for a few seconds and then would get busy in planning a 'leg-pulling ceremony' for your paraglider son and Captology-stricken daughter.

Even if some children are born to save the world, their parents make lives of us lesser mortals miserable. The 'trash can treatment' my parents bestow on me after meeting these highly gifted children or their boastful parents is gut-wrenching.

'My colleague's son got into an Ivy League college. He gave a Ted Talk on solar energy usage. Why don't you join a public speaking class and search about renewable energy resources?'

'Your cousin in Jalandhar has made some YouTube video. He sent me the link (which he has obviously sent to me as well). Why don't you show your creativity?'[54]

---

[52] Symbolic Systems is an academic programme at Stanford University with an interdisciplinary concentration on 'the science of the mind', including courses in computer science, linguistics, philosophy and psychology.

[53] Captology is a new field of study in the design, theory and analysis of persuasive technologies; http://captology.stanford.edu/about/what-is-captology.html

[54] This is called 'Salience Effect', where one conveniently interprets a specific attribute of a person to be responsible for his success or failure; http://psychology.iresearchnet.com/social-psychology/social-cognition/salience/

You want us to do what you think other children are doing. Not only that, we are expected to excel in those areas too where you sucked.

Although, if you could not learn to run or swim even to save your life, we are expected to ace these activities too!

'I don't know how to run but sports are so important. Don't make the mistake that I made. Swim every week and run every day,' comes the diktat.

You motivate us to compete with others in everything—sports, arts, music and, of course, academics.

Who gave you the idea that competition motivates? You talk to me about the toppers when I am close to the bottom. I play tennis at college level and you use Andy Murray to fire me up. I end up losing all my steam.

Rather than observing my position in any list of performances, you benchmark me against the best.

'If he can do it, you can too.'

I can certainly beat the person just above me in the list or two notches above me. But your eyes only look at the top and your heart desires to see my name there. I wish I was everyone's favourite just like I am yours.

Social scientists say that in a basketball game, the losing team has 7 per cent more chance to win if they are behind only by one point at the break time. They are more motivated to lose that tiny gap and they try three times harder. But it is only true when the gap is merely one point. As the gap increases, chances of the losing team to get ahead decreases.

I can win over the person who is not far ahead of me. If I look at the winner at the far end, it soars my pessimism. Next time, you intend to motivate me to do better, don't swoon over the topper. Look at the one in the middle or the bottom.

Parents suck when they obsess over our performances on a daily basis. Do they realize that their children love them without knowing whether they are a topper somewhere or not? We don't expect them to do well every quarter. We don't pressurize them to get an appraisal. We don't judge them when they get a pink slip.

A new study[55] shows that success depends more on personality than intelligence. After combing through data on IQ scores, standardized test results, personality assessment and grades for thousands of people in Britain, America and the Netherlands, researchers concluded that raw IQ scores do not guarantee worldly success. 'Valedictorians do not make future visionaries', they say. Thanks to economist James Heckman, who says that personality traits like conscientiousness, or a personality trait marked by diligence, perseverance and self-discipline leads to financial success, not grades.

The funniest problem is that our parents push us to be obedient and do everything virtuous to be a 'good' child. Our teachers prepare us to follow every rule and ace every exam to be a 'good' student. You persuade us to do everything like a perfect follower and then expect that we will lead and change the world. Really? You sow rosemary and expect roses—that's naïvely funny.

You expect us to get good grades and try all the possible ways to achieve it—hire tutors, teach us yourself, do our homework and nag us no end. A US-based National Longitudinal Study

---

[55] http://www.inc.com/jessica-stillman/success-depends-more-on-personality-than-intelligence-new-study-shows.html

of Adolescent Health tested 1,700 children—a mix of identical twins, fraternal twins, siblings, cousins and non-relatives. It showed that if you are in the 80th percentile of your class, expect your identical twin (even if you have never met him) to be in the 71st. They performed well not because of upbringing but because of their genes.

So, your expectations from us should correspond more with the quality of your genes and less with your gruelling efforts to teach us. Don't freak out if I fail to top my class or do not make to the fanciest college. I will figure it out, a little easier though, if you keep faith in me.

Look at me and then set your expectations from me. Please do not look at yourself or others to set expectations for me. How about giving 'my future' a break?

REASON 26

You Resemble a Gorilla

Whenever I meet someone for the first time who has known my parents from before, their first reaction is, 'You look exzhactly like your Mom.' If they like my Dad more, they confidently remark, 'She resembles Sir so much.'

If I agree with both sets of people; I should infer that I resemble both of them which means they resemble each other.

When children are toddlers, everyone loves to play this resemblance game, though it is a given—our common genes, duh! A true surprise would be when I resembled a gorilla rather than my parents.

My mother finds me very similar to my Dad in my attitude and behaviour while my Dad finds me to be annoying and rude. Both are right.

But if I resemble you guys more than myself, your genes are responsible for how I think and behave.

Next time, you shout at me for being lazy or short-tempered, I will sing, 'It's all in the genes.'

All our efforts to differentiate ourselves are generally disliked by you because you love to see us as an extension of yours or as an extension of your extension. You want us to look like you, dress like you and eat what you like to cook. You want us to be conformists but as we start defining ourselves as unique and distinct, you start feeling left out and cheated. Though you decide to go on a foreign vacation because all your colleagues are doing the same, you choose a unique location and keep it a secret. You desire to be different from others but you expect your children to be your reflection.

Why do you try hard to keep a visible association thread running? A respondent wrote that his father wants him to 'fit in' with the family but 'stand out' in the society.

Your children should be strikingly similar to you but drastically distinct from others.

Parents promote association in different ways within family:

- **By labelling.** 'The elder one is the brainy one while the younger one is the funny one.' Hence, the younger one is more like his father. These labels sometimes stick for life, becoming an expectation. A respondent observed, 'Since my parents branded me as funny, they didn't like it when I got irked by some comment of theirs. "But we thought you were funny", was their answer.' Their labelling positions us like a brand.
  If it is a sauce, it has to be hot and sour. Similarly, if it is me, my responses have to be funny.
- **By pointing at similarity in physical attributes.** 'The elder one's eyes are my exact replica while her hair is like her father.' Many contributors to Quora had mixed feelings about it. Many felt connected to their parents through such association, while many, who did not share a happy relationship with their parents, resented the resemblance and constant mention of it by people around.
- **By finding temperamental and habitual association.** 'My son is impatient like his grandfather. My daughter sleeps just like her brother does.' How observational! I

fail to understand how these repetitive statements help anyone. Not only this, a friend told me recently that his father often says that he performs well in Maths because he has taken on him.

- **Physical resemblance and temperamental similarities are extended into the realm of career choices too.** Parents wish to have at least one child follow in their footsteps especially if they own a business of any kind. It hurts them a lot if no one wants to continue their legal practice or work at their sweet shop.
- **If one sibling succeeds at a particular vocation, the other one is directly or indirectly motivated to follow suit.** You love to promote association among siblings. Since you guys try hard to make us look/behave/be like at least someone in the family, it motivates us to be different. If my brother is a sportstar, that path is already taken. So, I try to study or doodle or dance. Your love for association drives us towards differentiation. If I also like to swim or dance like my elder sibling, I will always have to compete with him/her. Not only this, I will always hear that I followed him/her. If one of us becomes a champion at the national level, the other one's life will be surrounded with negative attention all the time. Even if I love to swim or dance, it is better that I take up soccer or doodling.

Though it is a common occurrence in India to have at least one child following the career of his/her parent, a recent research showed the same for people world over.

Approved by Facebook, data scientists Ismail Onur Filiz

and Lada Adamie researched the networking site and used data from 5.6 million people to show that children follow their parents more in jobs such as of nurses, lawyers and scientists.[56]

The research revealed that a nurse's daughter was 3.75 times more likely to become a nurse than the rest of the population. A fifth of daughters whose mothers worked in office and administrative support choose the same career, twice the usual rate.

Not only this, a US census data revealed that 22 per cent of American men work for the same companies as their fathers. The corresponding figures in Denmark and Canada were 28 per cent and 40 per cent, respectively.[57]

This generational passing of the torch happens because the dinner table conversations in an architect's home revolve around why a building collapsed while a politician will discuss terrorism or corruption.

In my opinion, it is not coercive but it silently nudges us towards the familiar, the comfort zone career. Parents like it when their children make similar career choices because it gives them more ways to influence their lives.

A lawyer's son gets the best internships and job opportunities due to his father's network. An actor's son or daughter can afford more flops, a politician's son or daughter is born with a safe career. These parents suck because:

- They are making the path difficult for many deserving people.

---

[56] https://www.theatlantic.com/business/archive/2015/06/nepotism-mobility-same-jobs-fathers/395567/
[57] Ibid.

- They condition their children to think more about these specific careers and never motivate them to take risks or try out newer stuff. Industrialist parents get hurt when their children do not want to join their ventures.
- They want us to be different from others and similar to themselves. 'Accident called birth' perpetuates association whose fire is further stoked by parents. Children don't realize that they have freedom of will to choose a life without getting influenced by their parents' choices.

You imitate us to increase the association. Your language and dressing style changes according to our tastes. You include words like 'yolo', 'dude', 'legit' in your vocabulary along with funky clothes and accessories in your wardrobe. You wish to appear cool. You signal that you understand us.

We feel embarrassed because we see that you are trying too hard.

As you mix up with our friends and try to be one amongst us, we wish to move away. We might not say it in words and you, who are so observant otherwise, fail to read body cues or awkward silences.

Often, by the time you adopt to a craze that we swore by, we have already moved on. By the time you mastered dabbing, we were on to the mannequin challenge. As we saw more and more senior people take to dabbing, we felt like avoiding it completely.

Though the digital window has opened the world to us, it is not easy to brush aside associations that influence us unconsciously and constantly.

I am proud of my toothy smile and my 'fast and furious' temper which resembles my parents. It startles me though when they mention the similarities and differences between us all the time as if they are of my making. Would a gardener tend to an apple orchard in the same way as a berry bush? Would he appreciate a mango tree more than a watermelon plant? He would celebrate their uniqueness while keeping in mind their need for water, sunlight and manure.

How about parents highlighting our uniqueness rather than stressing on our similarities and discounting our differences?

REASON 27

My Name is Spy...Digital Spy!

One day, a classmate came to school wearing a disgusted look on his face. Since he was one of the first ones to fill in my research questionnaire, he told me to add another question in it—'How do you feel when your parents trick you into checking your laptop?'

I gave an unimpressed look which translated into asking to elaborate.

He took a chair to sit, but as he was so agitated, he decided to pace the corridor instead. 'Last evening, my dad came to me with his colleague's story who checked the history of his subordinate's desktop to prove that he should be paid a salary by online shopping companies and not their organization.

'My dad gave a vivid description of how his colleague pressed a few keys and out came all the hidden carcasses.

'Then he excitedly asked me if I could teach him how to check the history of someone's online activities on his/her desktop. I puffed up at the mere thought of being a tutor to my dad, even for a minute.

'And guess what! He used the acquired knowledge to check the history from my laptop only.'

This cracked me up.

'How did you come to know?'

'He forgot to close the tab after reading its contents.'

'He was only applying the newly gained knowledge,' I said, attempting to diffuse the situation.

My friend was seriously irked and he continued, 'He doesn't know about the Incognito mode![58] I will go home and tell him that such tactics will not work.'

'Don't think too much in to it. Parents get worried that we might be talking to strangers or watching offensive stuff or wasting time playing games.' I tried to calm him down, after all, I had three classes with him that day.

'I think he did not close the tab because he was so disappointed to not find anything objectionable. He missed a chance of showing his authority and scolding me. I can bet that I will find more explosive stuff on his phone if I sneak into it.'

Now, that was pizza for my starving brain, I mean, food for thought.

Parents keep an eye on us digitally in two ways:

- **Direct check.** They keep a tab on our phones, laptops or tablets by signing in periodically. Some smart parents claim of having some apps through which they know about the activities of our phones if our data plans are in their names.[59]
- **Indirect check.** They are connected to our social media network which keeps them abreast with all our posts.

Parents keep direct check on our digital devices because:

- **They feel that children are too young to use**

---

[58]Incognito is a Google support method that helps the user to browse the Web privately and the activity is not saved; https://www.thrillist.com/entertainment/nation/what-is-incognito-mode-google-chrome

[59]https://www.huffingtonpost.in/entry/how-to-track-your-kids-without-them-knowing-youre-on-their-tail_us_55afaff1e4b07af29d56f544

computers and smartphones on their own. An independent study by MAIT & KPMG says that 53 per cent of Indian parents introduce their children to computers at 5 to 10 years of age.[60] I see 7 to 8 year olds around me with phones in their hands and earphones in their ears.

Though I got my first phone in Class X (that too because of my grandmom. Thank you Dadi. My parents bought an iPhone for her which she didn't want and it fell in my craving lap). I was certainly the last one in my class to have it.

Most parents buy these devices early because they get tired of giving their phones to their children. To keep their phones safe and protected, they agree to buy a phone for their child, just like any other toy. Many parents buy it early because they feel pressurized by their children who argue that all their friends already have phones.

Parents play a helpless victim card and hand over a phone too early to their children. 'The children are so pushy these days. Also, they feel left out when others have a phone and they don't', is their excuse.

Do you want us to buy that excuse? Nah, not working. You guys have more power over us than you want to believe.

I think you are succumbing to social validation because you have not woken up to the severe behavioural addiction these devices are causing.

---

[60]http://www.huffingtonpost.in/2015/06/12/what-indian-pc-users want_n_7551024.html

It is not very wise to give me car keys just because I claim that my friends have them and then, either worry incessantly about my safety, or hop in the car with me all the time.

- **Parents check our digital devices directly to propagate 'deterrence'.** Parents want us to be scared of their surprise intrusions the same way as some countries show their nuclear bomb authority to deter others.

Why it sucks is because you question us about non-existing breaches. I get shouted at if music is being downloaded on my laptop. 'Is this how you study?' comes the arrow.

I get glared at if I send pictures of my homework to my friend.

'Why are you helping others? Don't be a show off', comes another arrow.

Parents keep indirect check on our digital engagement through our social media presence by following us. They do so because:

- **They want to be a part of our virtual world, so that they don't miss out on any digital landmark of our lives.** A friend's mother sent him FB friend requests relentlessly till he accepted more out of exasperation than guilt. Now, she gives him offline comments on every online post like, 'Why did you post your picture from "No Shave November"? You resemble a bear' or 'Why did you post a video where you are dancing to a Honey Singh song? Preposterous!'

- Why do you want to understand the relevance of every status update? Once I wrote, 'This is the start of something beautiful', as my status, which is the lyrics of a famous Ed Sheeran song, and you got all charged up to discover this new start.

- **They continuously worry about our digital image.** They hate our 'pout' DPs (display pictures for the uninitiated), they fail to understand our Snapchat stories and worry that we are offending someone, somewhere. Just as the Abercrombie & Fitch guys were worried about their brand image when Sorrentino, a participant on *Jersey Shore* TV show wore their clothes,[61] they get extremely cautious about our image when we post candid pictures or loud, funny videos. Everyone was running to a Coldplay concert held recently in Mumbai.[62] I was one of them, too. (I love those guys!) My mother checked pictures and status updates of ten friends of mine before approving the pictures that I wanted to upload. The amateur Byomkesh Bakshi[63] in you really sucks.

You are not only worried about whom I spend my offline time with, you are also concerned whom I post pictures with, and whom I tag in my posts.

You do not want me to do anything that gets me identified with the under-achieving, reckless peers

---

[61] https://www.theguardian.com/media/2011/aug/17/jersey-shore-situation-abercrombie-fitch

[62] Coldplay is a popular English alternative rock band. It performed in Mumbai in November 2016. The highly priced tickets were the talk of the town; https://www.firstpost.com/entertainment/coldplays-mumbai-concert-reviewed-this-ones-not-a-hymn-to-the-weekend-3118776.html

[63] Byomkesh Bakshi is a popular Bengali fictional detective created by Sharadindu Bandyopadhyay.

or notorious celebrities. To achieve your objective of keeping my digital image sanitized, you mercilessly intrude in my online and offline life.

First, please hold on to your ground and do not let us get a phone like a toy. Please do not litter the house with your digital garbage. Most of the children get a phone when the dad buys a new phone—which could be as frequent as every year. 'My dad bought a new phone, so my mom got his old phone and I got my mom's'—say many of my friends.

How about not making it a practice?

Second, please cultivate 'mutual trust'. A mutual access to our phones makes us accountable. It is not a 'tell' unequation, it becomes a 'show-and-tell' equation.

Let us have a digital level playing field and you would not need to sneak in my dark room for a search operation.

If you become a digital stalker on social media, I would feel horrible.

My mom is turning into a strategist rather than a stalker now.

A friend of hers told her about a brilliant student who got accepted to a top US college but was denied admission after being found to have made some racial comments online.

She simply shared the story and left. The ball has been in my court since then.

REASON 28

Yesterday Ended Last Night

My mom and I took a short vacation to Goa recently. The trip was memorable for two reasons. First, we developed the outline of this book on this trip.

Second, we had a unique experience. The hotel manager showed us into a newly refurbished room. It was so fresh that we could smell the paint. Since we had arrived on a hot afternoon, we crashed immediately. Two hours later, I got up in a room full of water. Everything was floating.

We were immediately shifted to another room. When we enquired in the evening about what went wrong, the manager sheepishly said, 'There was some glitch in the bathroom area. We sincerely apologize for the inconvenience.'

My ever-curious mother prodded further, 'There was some major leakage from the bathroom wall. What kind of renovation did you guys do?'

'Actually madam, they forgot to change the leaking pipe only, which had initiated the whole process of refurbishing in the first place. The pipe burst today, thus causing so much chaos.'

I wondered about our fascination for 'change'.

As children, we are bundles of repetition, as well as novelty.

When we are young, you get tired of feeding us, rocking us and watching over us. It is monotonous for a while but then, we grow up and bring novelty. From stationed at one place, we start running around. From obeying, we start defying. From listening, we start debating.

Do you see variety? Do you experience novelty? While we transform from our terrible twos into turbulent teens, you remain the same (at least, in your response to us). You try to baby us and instruct us in the same way. When our responses change, you say, 'When you were young, you were so good!'

Do you realize how boring it is for us to meet the parents who have pledged not to evolve. Living with you is like having the same soup every day. While, for you, living with us is like getting to taste a new dish each time you go to a restaurant.

Imitating our language (slangs), trying to fit in with our friends is not 'changing'. We are not looking for superficial congruence. We want adaptability—a sort of frequency-changing switch that you guys used to love winding on antique radio sets. You guys need some acute observation and listening skills to tune into the station with the right frequency. You guys need similar skills to tune into our dynamic lives.

It further gets hard for you guys to change the gears midway because you get so attached to the investment already made while we excel at dropping a class and picking a new one.

'Don't leave a class after taking it for three months. You have already spent thirty hours and our hard-earned money.'

'How can you scrap your project/painting now? You have already finished the ground work.'

You all suffer from sunk-cost fallacy while we don't want to waste two more years just because we have already wasted three months. We can't think of working through a project in which we have already lost interest during the prep time.

When you want us to continue with something that we have lost interest in, it is because of any of these reasons:

- You have spent enough on that activity or course or project that leaving it now makes you feel at a loss. You don't think about the money that you will still pay which will add to that loss.
- You don't want to be known as parents who raised inconsistent children. For you, having inconsistent children is similar to having an 'on-time' train journey in Indian hinterland. The credibility is at stake.
- Indian parents suffer from perennial fear that their children might miss out on something very crucial. Whatever we decide to forego becomes extremely valuable to you only because we decided to abandon it. You want us to do everything possible. Leaving something and that too midway is like missing out on Wimbledon while visiting London.

After finishing law school, when Gretchen Rubin told her dad that she wanted to become a writer, her dad supported her.[64] Rubin later appreciated this gesture of her father and felt grateful for his unstinted belief in her. 'There comes a time in every parent's life when they need to switch from being an adviser to a cheerleader,' shared her dad.

Paint, once used, cannot remain as fresh as it was in the can. Me, after coming out of your secure womb, cannot remain the same. You need to stay ahead of me and hence evolve at a faster pace. The future will NOT resemble the past.

Everyone would agree that it is the 'most challenging' for

---

[64]Gretchen Rubin is the author of several books, including the *New York Times* bestsellers, *Better Than Before*, *The Happiness Project* and *Happier at Home*; https://gretchenrubin.com/

your generation for not only witnessing but also adapting to very frequent winds of change. As children, your lives were spent in the 'programming era' which was not very different from the previous times. As mobile phones and Internet connectivity expanded, your youth experienced the pangs of change in every aspect of your lifestyle. By the time we were born, you were standing on the threshold of the twenty-first century which has been a witness to the fastest rate of change. No other generation would ever see it all—from trunk calls to in-flight phone calls, from hide-and-seek to blue whale.

The way you guys need to adapt as parents and as professionals is excruciatingly challenging. You need to get unstuck from your past because you cannot borrow much from your parents' experiences. Our 'appy' lives demand so much adaptive behaviour from you.

You cannot fall back on anything familiar and hence your anxiety levels soar and your confidence levels plummet. Accelerated anxiety makes you either extra cool or extra controlling. Crushed confidence makes you either helpless or defensive. I can notice the tired look on your face from the corner of my eye.

Last year, Megan Evans, a 14-year-old in the UK, ended her life after being bullied on Snapchat. Parents are being exposed to new challenges and the only way to face them is to be aware about their existence.[65]

Life was much easier in the '80s and the '90s when there were no mobile phones, social media, TV, Web shows for instant streaming and even Pokémon Go. Parents might

---

[65]http://www.dailymail.co.uk/news/article-5440533/Parents-demand-answers-school-daughters-death.html

complain that their parenting challenges have proliferated, whining won't help much. What will help is an attitude to quickly adapt to the changes by tweaking your responses.

Though technology has caused change in all the nooks and crannies of our lives, the fundamentals of relationships, of emotional and creative fulfilment cannot change.

Parents are a part of actors as well as the audience in our lives. As actors, they are active doers, and as audience, they are passive observers and thinkers. Some parents are merely focusing on the actor–doer piece and hence our trying to keep up with the whirlwind of change without assessing whether all the change needs to be devoured or not.

Some parents are merely focusing on the observer–thinker piece and hence are only commenting on the changing scenario without accepting that they will need to own many of the changes.

How about joining both the pieces so that you guys can accept the needed changes but at the same time warn us from getting carried away in the name of change?

How about creating as well as curating an innovative but balanced lifestyle which uses technology but doesn't get used by it, which picks up programming but doesn't give up poetry?

Also, change means a change in the core not in the crust. A change in the core means that you evolve from being a self-righteous parent to a vulnerable one who is ready to accept that s/he could be wrong. How about adding some vulnerability to your self-righteousness?

REASON 29

Diamonds and Dirt

A parent gets angrier than any other regular person. Each parent is guilty of treating their children as a doormat at some point in time.

Children are the softest targets for all the pent-up emotions. Anger accumulated during different exchanges with a boss, an in-law, a spouse or any helpless situation comes out on the child, even for a minor slip up.

A mother's anger is pretty extensive while a father's anger is generally intensive. Mother's outbursts are a recollection of several past mistakes compounded by her anger towards those over whom she can't show her authority.

A father's anger is generally intense but focused on the mistake at hand.

Parents have a lot of authority over young children, which allows them to get angry comfortably and fearlessly. Verbal attacks or physical abuse can leave permanent scars. No justification that we drove you crazy or your situation was such can make the wrong a right.

Parents lose it more with their children because there are many childhood memories of helplessness and pain which sharpen the present axe of anger. The pain and anger influenced by you will make us lose our temper in a similar way when we will become parents.

This is so unfair. How about breaking this linear path of pain handed over by each parent to his/her children?

Have you heard of these five favourite words of every parent: *'The problem with you is...'* These can be found at any location inside a parents' brain.

When I did not have friends, the problem with me was: 'You are a loner.'

When I started making friends, the problem with me was: 'You are just about friends.'

When you shout at me and I look at you, you say: 'Why are you staring at me? The problem with you is that you are a defiant kid. You have no courtesy. Don't stare.'

When you shout at me and I look down, you say: 'Why are you acting innocent? The problem with you is that you are a shammer. You have no honesty. Don't look down.'

When you shout at me and I look in some other direction, you say: 'Why are you ignoring me? The problem with you is that you are ignorant and indifferent. You have no shame. Look at me.'

Your ambiguous statements have one staple ingredient: *'The problem with you is...'* You use these words irrespective of what we do.

A respondent wrote, 'My elder brother shifted to another city for work. Because he lived alone, he would cook for himself. Then my mom went to visit him. She told him, "Don't bother to cook till I am here. Let me do that."

When she came back, she complained to him over the phone, 'I don't know what you will eat in my absence. You never cooked anything.'

Should I be using, *'The problem with you is...'* for you?

Last year, I heard about the concept of Transactional

Analysis[66] and finally figured out why parents and children don't understand each other.

Why did they not teach us about this analysis as soon as we were born? Rather than pushing us to master alphabets and numbers, we should have been trained to figure out the P-A-C ego states.

Every individual has three ego states—Parent, Adult and Child—inside him/her. At any given point in time, he could be communicating from any of the states and nobody knows how to fathom that.

A 5-year-old wants to go play ball on a beach.

Day one. Parent (from Parent ego state): Don't go in the sand. A no means no.

Day two. Parent (from the Adult ego state): Have fun. Be safe.

Day three. Parent (from the Child ego state): Can you give me the ball? Let's play.

Think about this 5-year-old who realizes that instead of parents, he has been handed over a pack of assorted moods. How is he going to respond to this?

Parents are highly animated and opinionated beings and hence keep jumping ego states on the trampoline of daily routine. We need mastery over this psychological condition, called Transactional Analysis, to understand this mood jugglery of parents.

They stay in the *feeling* child state and behave like children when we make them emotional and nostalgic.

They move to the *teaching* parent state when we need advice or guidance, which is all the time.

---

[66]Thomas A. Harris. 2004. *I'm OK-You're OK*. New York: HarperCollins.

Occasionally, they invite themselves to be in the *thinking* adult state.

I come across this trapeze performance by my mother every other day. I have just entered the last year of my school. My mom suddenly bursts into tears thinking I will leave home soon. The next minute, she is hollering for the thirteenth time since morning to make me organize my study table (which is fairly neat in my view). By the time I reach for my headphones to save me from her fourteenth shout-out, she maturely pulls a chair next to me to discuss my university choices.

When they keep shifting their ego states, we need to match up to be called cultured and nice. It is like shifting from bhangra to bhajans to Beyoncé!

If I flunk a test, my Mom will_____.

'Get mad', 'take it easy', 'get into silent mode' or 'none of the above', can be the options. My answer is, 'it depends'.

If my friend along with whom I prepared, passed the test, she will get mad.

If she read the news of a boy committing suicide due to examination pressure, she will take it easy.

If she was a topper herself and I have always been a let-down, she will get into the silent zone.

It will be a completely different story with my Dad.

If he had a stressful day at office, he will take it easy. He needs peace and comfort, at least at home.

If he had a pleasant day at work, he will choose to get mad. Some conflict is healthy and welcome after all.

If he is truly sad or disillusioned with life, he will soothe himself by staying silent.

My flunking the test is a non-entity here.

Petulant parents treat us like diamonds as well as dirt. They shower me with their attention that is disguised in instruction, advice and so on. They ignore me with the same intensity when I fall short of their escalating expectations.

Their positive emotions 'inspire' me, but their negative emotions 'infect' me. Whether I like it or not, whether I want it or not, I catch many of their thoughts, emotions and behaviours.

More of 'diamond behaviour' turns me into a diamond who behaves with dignity with others. More of 'dirt behaviour' turns me into dirt which behaves with rudeness with others.

Your temper trapeze torments us because it is arbitrary, emotional and confusing.

How about being a little predictable and plausible?

Parenting according to your mood is an inconsistent way of treating us.

Listen, reflect and react.

Please, let it be about me, not you.

REASON 30

The TINA Factor

When I am hungry, I have a pizza or paratha to get the job done—to satiate my hunger.

When I want a new haircut, I contact a hair expert to get this job done.

I choose the job, I choose the doer of the job and I get impacted by the job.

When I am conceived, two individuals choose the job, do the job but I am the one who gets impacted the most.

After my birth, their job as individuals gets done and their job as parents gets started.

But I have no choice in deciding the doers of the job. I can't even say much about the quality of the job that they do. The *TINA—There Is No Alternative*—factor rules our childhood.

A leader becomes a leader when there is someone to follow.

A parent becomes a parent when there is someone to nurture, love, encourage and guide—a child in short.

A child who needs love, nurturing, encouragement and guidance makes you a parent. For how long do you remember this?

For some parents, kids are toys. For some, kids are trophies. For some parents, they are a blessing. For some, they are a burden.

We, as children, are clueless about the type of cards we are dealt by destiny. No child is the writer of his/her story's first page. Parents write it. Our parents, who are young and naïve, take the parenting plunge without any planning. They don't dwell on it enough.

I don't know if my parents and me are a perfect fit.

Marriage is a gamble, they say. Being born is a bigger gamble.

Osho wisely mentioned about having a 'commune' to raise children, as he believed that young parents were not competent enough to raise new lives.

We are your specimen for live experiments. You do things for us based on your past experiences. 'I learnt Sanskrit when I was five. It is good to learn a new language at an early age. So you should also learn some language.'

You persuade us to do things that you enjoy. 'It is fun to read comics. So, you must read.'

You influence us emotionally to do things that you wanted to do but couldn't. 'I always wanted to learn how to play a musical instrument but there was no opportunity or resources. I am giving you the opportunity to learn whichever instrument you like. You must learn.'

Thus, I become a part of the experiments run by you. The first decade of my life is totally TINA. The second decade is a struggle for me for not letting it become TINA.

You decide the time and order of my birth. I have no say in deciding anything about my own birth. I can't choose if I want to be the firstborn. I might end up being low in the hierarchy.

You call us demanding and picky. You call us choosy and rigid but our life begins at such a helpless and 'choice-less' note.

Psychologists say that firstborns have a high chance of becoming senators, doctors and lawyers. They are practical decision-takers who get a lot of attention from their parents.[67]

Firstborns get more joyful engagement[68] in the first two years of their lives with their mothers and, hence, are more driven and successful. If I am the second child, you have already reduced my chances of succeeding in life because you will neither have the time nor the energy to shower me with all the attention and affection I deserve. And in many Indian societies, if the first- and second-born are girls, parents may get enticed by the idea of bringing a third child to life! The quality of my life now tethers around this 'to-be born' who will take away all the attention and affection upon the virtue of being a boy. If I get another sister, the whole family gets overcast by gloom for quite some time, may be a lifetime.

A recent research shows that children born in the middle, like Mark Zuckerberg, Bill Gates and Lord Alan Sugar, are more likely to become CEOs. They develop traits like competitiveness, flexibility and diplomacy as they have to fight for attention all the time. If you decide to have more than two children, only then do I stand a chance of getting the middle seat in the birth order. Also, skills that I acquire to survive as a middle child become my personality traits for life. This is how your decisions chart the course of our lives. I will most likely end up being an engineer or an astronaut if I am the firstborn for no fault of mine![69]

---

[67]Jeffrey Kluger. 2011. *The Sibling Effect: What the Bonds Among Brothers and Sisters Reveal About Us.* New York: Riverhead Books.
[68]Joseph Burgo. 2012. *Why Do I Do That? Psychological Defence Mechanism and the Hidden Ways They Shape Our Lives.* Chapel Hill, NC: New Rise Press.
[69]http://epaperbeta.timesofindia.com/Article.aspx?eid=31804&articlexml=Middle-children-30-more-likely-to-be-CEOs-1604201 7015048

The child at the end of the birth order generally meets parents who are so exhausted and burdened that s/he has to virtually raise herself/himself up.

I may turn out to be an entrepreneur because you planned my arrival in the middle order.

I may turn out to be an artist if I am given the last position in the birth order.

You may laugh at me or loathe me for this thought. It becomes very difficult for me to warm up to couples who have two daughters followed by a son. Their gender bias is grossly visible. I fail to understand the plight of a child who knows that his/her parents have killed some of their unborn children. How difficult it would be to live with them. To make it easy to live with such parents, they learn to change their frame of reference. To dilute the drudgery, they accept it as a social compulsion. They kill their sensitivity to match your insensitivity. To live with you peacefully, they accommodate by silencing their conscience.

Please don't blame me if I want to shun my studies and want to listen to a Beethoven or Badshah. Rather, I reserve the right to put it on my 'birth order'.

I do not know why human babies are born dumber than other animal babies. They need more support from parents than other species and this dependent beginning casts us into a mould of helplessness. Each parent gets stuck in that mould. How about quickly realizing that human babies are meant to outgrow that 'unfinished infant phase' very quickly?

How about helping us to move from 'helpless' to 'self-help' mode? How about equipping us to be our own masters rather than moulding us so that you can continue to be our masters?

You are already embossed on our genes. How about giving us a few alternatives so that we do not fall in the category of 'as helpless as babies' even when we grow up?

REASON 31

Observation Is a Dying Art. You Are the Living Example

A 5-year-old went up to his father, 'Papa, what is sex?'

The father was startled and slapped the boy.

The boy went to the school the next day and returned with a letter:

'Kindly fill this form and send with your child', read the letter.

One of the unfilled entry on the form read—Sex: Male/Female.

Three cheers for the father!

My life experiences do not include driving a four-wheeler yet. I occupy, literally and figuratively, the back seat. Those who are experts in occupying the back seat will vouch for me when I say that we can see many things far more clearly than the driver who fails to be 100 per cent attentive. Drivers pay attention everywhere; they are versatile rubberneckers but they do not know what is going on in the back seat. Tom Vanderbilt, in his book, *Traffic*[70], says that, 'Most crashes happen on dry roads, on clear, sunny days to sober drivers when they FEEL SAFE. Drivers rarely mess up at dangerous places like narrow roads or steep turns.' Parents are no different than drivers. While considering themselves as drivers of our lives, their self-

---

[70]Tom Vanderbilt. 2008. *Traffic: Why We Drive the Way We Do (and What It Says About Us)*. New York: Knopf Doubleday.

assurance and over-confidence mask their eyes. They see, but do not observe. Seeing and observing are different things. You see your children every day, but then, you see millions of objects every day; you don't observe most of them. You believe that you understand us. But the contrary is truer on most of the days. Your brain is wired into the to-do list while you wake me up with an automated kiss, your eyes surf through my face and your phone on the breakfast table. Your mind waves a goodbye to me before your mouth does. When we meet again in the day, you listen to the words I utter but you cannot read what I leave unsaid. When I try to talk about how I feel, you guys standardize it as *natural.*

Any kind of peer pressure, bullying or anger issues are either exaggerated or my fault. You don't like to discuss my pain points with counsellors or teachers as it makes you feel inadequate.

You ignore the signs of low self-esteem, because, firstly, you have no time. Secondly, you reckon it is just a phase. Thirdly, children exaggerate most of their experiences—according to you.

You never acknowledge that you might be pushing us to the wall. You never notice that someone else might be dangerously playing with us. Many a times, it is too late by the time you manage to interpret and assimilate what we were trying to convey.

We could be a vulnerable lot. We hide our fears and failures because we are scared of 'how you will react'. We are scared of disappointing you but you see the outcomes and never observe our intentions.

Our feelings, stressors and fears crave for your undivided attention. After a while, we assume that we are not important, we accept that you will never understand.

If we do not barge into a visible mess, life moves on. If we land up in any unwarranted situation, you will be shocked because you never saw that coming.

To be silent and strategic observers, parents need to be as alert as a police dog. They need to be sensitive to sound, taste, view, touch and smell—any change in your sensory experience around us is a red flag. They need to underplay their emotions to observe us effectively.

Many parents suffer from the Slippery Slope bias.[71]

A respondent shared that he and his friend were studying at a top law school of the country. He was always a topper of his class and made it to the law school in the first attempt while his friend was his senior from school and was academically average and made it to the college in the third attempt.

As is usual, they both messed up in the first semester. They studied less, partied hard and wasted themselves.

When both the boys went home, the parents of the respondent saw a big and sudden change in him. They immediately took him to task and gave him a stern warning, meanwhile, his friend's parents failed to see much difference in his behaviour.

When there is a steep fall, it is easier to get noticed. If the fall occurs in small increments—on a slippery slope—it might go unnoticed. That is why the boy who was an average performer did not get pulled up by his parents because his

---

[71] A Slippery Slope bias refers to a relatively small first step that leads to a chain of related events culminating into some significant negative effect; https://www.logicallyfallacious.com/tools/lp/Bo/LogicalFallacies/162/Slippery-Slope

(deteriorating) performance was on a slippery slope.

A sudden non-alignment, a striking change in behaviour gets noticed easily, but gradual transgressions and minor but continuous changes in behaviour can go unnoticed.

Even when parents see some alarming instances, they do not dig deep because they feel that every child does things like that. When they see their children clicking pictures of every minor event of their daily lives, or when they notice their children returning home late in the night with wobbly legs, they do not raise red flags because they feel that this is the new normal.

Many children share their angst and anxieties with my mom. She listens to them with so much attention and empathy that I get crazily jealous. It seems like she is their mom too and, with all honesty, I admit that I love her as a human but it annoys me to no end when she is so loving to other children.

What she observes as an outsider, their parents overlook as insiders. She often says that the seeds of any disease are sown much earlier than the symptoms which show sporadically before becoming clearly visible.

Parents can use their observations to write algorithms to predict their kids' actions and behaviour the way retail companies observe our behaviour to predict our buying preferences.

Observation is a dying art. You are the living example. How about walking every evening with me into the day that just went by? How about secretly observing me while I am doing nothing

in particular? It will give you signs that even I am not aware of.

How about conducting a simple '5 Whys' test whenever you see a change in our behaviour or life patterns? The test will give you various insights as you keep peeling layer after layer of our personalities with each 'why'. Throwing a glance at us is not enough. Read between the lines, listen to our silence. Touch us. Smell US. And...you will find us.

REASON 32

Who Moved My Creativity?

As a child, I have a distinct memory of hearing 'no' from my parents for three things:

- When I would walk backwards.
- When I would not get out of my school uniform after coming home.
- When I would add salt to chocolates.

I fail to understand why they would restrict me from walking backwards (who knows I would have invented a new sport and become a champion!).

There is no way that they can convince me even now that changing into home clothes is mandatory. My mother ran after me like an armed soldier behind an enemy unless I changed.

She would hover over me to check if I sprinkled salt on my chocolate, as if it was cyanide not salt. Is saying 'no' a default setting with parents? Do they want to tell us that anything we say has to hit a firewall called 'no'?

Parents restrict us so often that we forget our freedom to think and act. Out of fear, they stop us from doing normal things like peeling a fruit or walking backwards. Out of social conformity, they don't allow boys to learn embroidery or girls to become drivers.

My father is an artist who is known for his creative pursuits. He enjoys being on stage and mesmerizes everyone with his words. At the moment, I have a real passion for photography and I work with my Mom on weekends as her digital manager. I recently shot a film at school and was excited to show the film to my parents. My name came on screen as the director of photography and I clapped. Mom was happy, but I could see that my Dad was not. He will not like me sharing it here but he felt that I would always remain a mere name on screen doing what I was doing. For him, working behind the camera was not a great idea.

Many friends who responded to my survey agreed that they were allowed to pursue creative and off-beat stuff till they were in primary classes. As the academic rigour grew, parents' 'love for a secure career' soared and rendezvous with creativity dwindled.

If we persist, they evaluate and compare us so blatantly that most of us chicken out and retreat to the common, tried and tested road to future. Constant restrictions, evaluations, surveillance and pressure to perform kills the creativity forever.

Our culture propagates conformity, compliance and congruence. Parents want children who conform to their world view, comply with their social-personal norms and are congruent with children who are accepted as propagators of intelligence and accomplishments. People like Kangana Ranaut and Ritesh Agrawal command respect as an actor and entrepreneur, respectively, but they would have given a lot of anxiety to their parents while breaking every granule of the walls of conformity, compliance and congruence.

A male contestant on a popular TV show recently showed his talent as a belly dancer. Decked in a skirt with tassels, he was appreciated for his form, technique, moves and an unconventional choice of dance form.[72] His backstory showed his father completely disapproving of his art: 'If my elder son goes out dancing in a ghagra, all the respect that I have earned in my life will be gone.'

Is it necessary and futuristic to use the same moulds for all of us? How about curbing your fears or at least zipping your lips when we wish to break some moulds?

Please don't transfer your fears and risk aversion to us. Please do not let your social validation rule our lives.

Creativity means uncertainty. Most parents hate uncertainty. They like it safe and secure for us.

- **Creativity means freedom.** Most parents detest the word. They like to exercise control over our choices by deciding for us, planning for us and implementing it for us.

  My mother is a great admirer of the late Justice Leila Seth, a woman who excelled in every domain of her life. The first woman to become a high court judge in India, she was the mother of three amazing children—a film-maker daughter, a Buddhism practitioner son and a very celebrated author son. She balanced her family priorities with her time-consuming professional commitments. For me, what sets her apart was her acceptance of her children as they were. She openly spoke about her son being homosexual and gave him all her love.[73]

---

[72]Eshan Hilal was a contestant on the show, *Dance Plus 3*.
[73]http://www.firstpost.com/living/the-gay-child-needs-more-love-leila-

- **Creativity means innovation.** Parents like it when someone else does it. They love risk-takers on TV, in newspapers. Since parents themselves become a cog in the machine, they lose their creative cells and, hence, cannot appreciate and encourage creativity among children. As they feel less moved by other's problems, their creativity lies dormant. However, children do not like to accept inadequacy and inefficiency as easily as elders.

  IGNITE competitions, organized by the National Innovation Foundation (NIF), bear testimony to it. A Class VII student, saw a real problem in her school. Younger students, short in height, faced problems while trying to drink water from the taps fixed at a higher spot. She came up with a simple idea of a water pipe with different taps at different inclined angles to serve children at different heights; three young boys have suggested ideas to create a censor that would put our computer screen off if our sitting posture is not right; a Class VIII student saw her grandfather facing problems while climbing the stairs using a walker. She suggested adding flexible front legs to the walker. A prototype of the improved walker model made by the Foundation was recently licensed to a company.[74]

- **Creativity means authenticity.** Still, most parents like social validation better. When parents accept

---

seth-on-vikram-seth-200154.html

[74] Anil K. Gupta. 2016. *Grassroots Innovation: Minds on the Margin Are Not Marginal Minds*. New Delhi: Random House. pp. 178–81.

their children with open arms and let them be, their creativity is at their best.

A parent can be the first custodian of our creativity, the first observer of our unique talents, the first cocoon to hold our reality forever.

Professor Anil Gupta, a propagator of 'grassroots innovation', says that the best place to be is where loving, living and learning intersect. Parents can provide us that place.

Unfortunately, money, violence and fame are more enticing powers than learning in adult life. Loving is equated with fulfilling duty in a family and living just happens.

Parents can create an environment of real problem-solving at a young age for children. Children, if given the opportunity, can solve real problems.

When young children are encouraged and expected to come up with solutions, they startle the so-called versatile product designers. Parents can easily become the creative hubs for society by encouraging their children to use their creative acumen for social improvement.

By forcing us to only excel in school exams, parents are guilty of making us insensitive and indifferent. I agree that our education system does not recognize such creative talents, but parents can certainly impact the collective consciousness of children by encouraging them to find solutions for various real-life issues. We, the children, can use the time that we are spending with our phones and laptops right now for the same.

We all are a reflection of God's creativity. How about letting his creativity flourish with freedom?

Parental interest, encouragement and expectation can grow a creative crop of children. How about giving it a try?

REASON 33

Pervasive Parentisms

Indian parents love a few thoughts the way we love pizza and noodles. Though these thoughts are deeply held beliefs for them, they are borderline lies for us.

Parents claim to be fair by reiterating that they love all their children equally. This is a blatant distortion.

Parents plead to be helpless by reiterating that their children do not listen to them. This is a deep deception.

Parents vouch to be motivating us by constant criticizing and comparing. This is a myth.

All these three widespread claims of parents are hyperboles that they cherish and we despise. Let's have a closer look at them.

i) **I love all my children equally.** Each parent who has more than one child has used this lie. It's similar to saying, 'We have many friends. But we have one best friend.'

When we were young, we were often asked, 'Whom do you love more—Mom or Dad?' I am sure that I always lied whenever I said 'Both'.

I always maintained a top five list of my family members and the index ranking followed my feelings towards that family member at that particular time. Both my parents were frequently in and out of this list based on their behaviour towards me and how it made me feel. Even if I tried, I could not hide it.

You tactfully make all of us believe that you are fair and

hence no child is your favourite. Since we all clamour to be that special favourite, all of us feel that you are inclined towards others.

Though this lie maintains the functionality of a family, each child feels short-changed.

There are disciplined moms who love their well-behaved child more. There are laidback moms who would secretly adore their laziest creation but it's always 'equality' on the masthead.

You live this lie forever, never budging from it.

If you have a high-achieving or well-behaved child, you would *'kick down'* the other one who receives less rating on your secret comparison meter. You will *'kiss up'* the high-performing child who has it in him to be a bestseller. You *'kiss up'* the socially acclaimed child and *'kick down'* the dark horse.

You guys pit us against each other and seal it with your eternal lie, 'We treat you both equally. We are comparing because this is how others will think about you.'

A respondent shared his amazing observation, 'If you have siblings born in the span ranging from 1990 to 2005, it is akin to the co-existence of a landline phone and a smartphone. If you have a sister born in 1990 while you were born in 1998, she would have missed out on some crucial things by a whisker while growing up.' Technological transformation has caused plenty of social alterations in the last two decades, resulting in strikingly different siblings and sibling relationships. The way we communicate and consume time has drastically changed in the two decades preceding and succeeding the year 2000. Parents are at a loss to completely fathom these changes. This respondent born in 1990 felt that her brother born in 2000 got a much relaxed parenting because information sharing increased and parents became more open.

Though it is human to like and admire someone more than the other, parents are expected to be superhumans and hence they try to deceive us by constantly clamouring about loving each child equally.

How about clearly communicating the qualities in each one of us that you admire and abhor? How about assessing us and clarifying that your opinions are specific to habits and events, while your love is beyond these.

At the end of the day, we must face the truth. We all have favourites. We all have different relationship wavelengths with different individuals. Till we are young, we crave be to the child you love the most. As we grow up, we will learn to get real.

ii) **My kids don't listen.** A lady shared this incident on a social networking site.[75] She went to a restaurant with her family. To her shock, she saw a 7- or 8-year-old child having a Breezer on the next table. She could not resist and approached the mother to inform her that the drink contains alcohol. She surely believed that the mother didn't know. The mother replied, 'I know. But what to do? Kids just don't listen.'

The drinks were ordered by adults and were being consumed by young children in their presence. The post had seventy-nine comments from women, out of which four women shared similar incidents where they saw kids as young as 2 drinking beer sitting in their mother's laps or children sipping drinks from their parents' glasses. If five women out of eighty come across these incidents,

---

[75]https://www.facebook.com/groups/firstmomsclub/permalink/1500919473293287/

it means 16 per cent of Indian parents might be those unfortunate parents who have been cursed with children 'who don't listen'.

Are we expected to sympathize with your misfortune? Should we accept that the clan of parents is really having a tough time due to these reckless, defiant children? Are you kidding?

Kids don't listen because:

- You are not saying things clearly and firmly. You say so much and so often and often don't mean it, that we get conditioned to pay no attention. You never enforce rules, completely indicating that every rule is malleable and is around to serve our whims.
- We see you. You do stuff that we copy and absorb. Did anyone ever tell you that we don't do what you say all the time but we certainly do, what you do. A friend of mine never knew that shoe laces are to be tied because his dad always kept them untied. (What a studly thing to do!)
- You postpone pain. You have perhaps never heard about future or future implications. You just want to have a good time today without tantrums of toddlers, without a display of crying, thumping, snatching or cussing children. You don't want to deal with our pestering power. Rather than nipping discipline issues in the bud, you are allowing a trail of ignorance and complacency to grow.

You let your toddler have alcoholic drinks, you let your tweens swear, you let your teens drive and then you seek sympathy for being rendered helpless.

Just because you don't know how to convey the difference between appropriate and inappropriate, just because you are short of patience to make us understand, you hide behind the 'children don't listen' poster.

You neither define nor correct unacceptable behaviour. A 'chalta hai' attitude creeps in your routine and you blame it on the present time when 'children don't listen.'

'An Ostrich Parent' becomes oblivious to the world of children and keeps harping about good old days. 'Past' and 'Present' begin and end with the same words but the middle journey has a different course which we need to acknowledge and pivot accordingly.

How about clearly formulating the family norms, communicating them to all family members and ensuring that everyone follows them? How about clearly mentioning the consequences of discipline breeches and sticking to them?

iii) **Our criticism is your motivation.** A Gadfly is a person who irritates or criticizes others to provoke them into action. Parents are gadflies to their children. They belittle them, irritate them, criticize them and challenge them. To add insult to injury, they garnish it with, 'We said so to motivate you to work harder. We wanted you to feel bad so that you promise yourself to be the best'. Socrates called himself a gadfly who provoked people to think and act. Ideally, the world needs such revolutionaries but two such revolutionaries in each home is a tad too much. Let 'live and let live' be our theme song.

Please clear your doubts. Your critical words merely motivate me to dislike you. My dopamine and your diatribe point towards the road to hell. Unnecessary fault-finding is a dampener and will remain one, your motivation rationale is a complete let-down.

If strangers or even friends laugh at us, we might want to work hard to prove them wrong. But we do not need constant criticizers at home who moonlight as gadflies. When we are already struggling on many fronts, your additional criticism merely adds to misery.

A friend shared his experience. 'I am always "laughed at" by my family members for avoiding studies. He applies a "study-repellent cream" every day, they say. In high school, I genuinely raised up my game and started studying seriously. My dad was planning a family trip during Diwali break and I had an exam just after the break, I refused to join them. My father forced me to come with them, they called me a spoilsport. Their main aim is to find fault in me, anyhow.'

Such daily bouts of fault-finding, making fun and demeaning comparison are stressors just like the Chinese water torture method, in which a drop constantly hits the same spot on one's head. How about motivating us by doing what you want us to do rather than using a dose of verbal venom on a daily basis?

REASON 34

Life in a 'Cell Phone'

This is the latest addition to my list. My generation is continuously blamed for being active on social media and being passive socially. We are berated for being glued to our screens, chatting non-stop and pouting.

You roll your eyes and spit out helpless words at our digital addiction. Wait. You check your phone in the middle of rolling your eyes and spitting these words.

Your 'friends list' on social networks exceeds mine. Your photo albums fill the digital domain more regularly than mine.

A recent survey[76] showed that adults (35–49 years) spend more time on social media than millennials. You tell us to use our time more efficiently but I am impressed by your efficiency. Not only this, you guys use these platforms to discuss the TV programmes that you follow. It might mean that you guys are watching more television than us.

Does this mean that you have all the free time at your disposal to squander away? I reckon that apart from instructing us on a daily basis, social media is your second-most loved pastime.

These are electronic babysitters more for you, than for us. Findings by Brandon T. McDaniel, assistant professor

---

[76]Nielsen Report, 'Times Trends', *The Times of India*, 30 January 2017, p. 15; http://epaperbeta.timesofindia.com/Article.aspx?eid=31804&articlexml=Gen-X-not-millennials-more-into-social-media-30012017015017

at Illinois State University, suggest an association between greater technology use by parents and potential relationship dysfunction between parents and children leading to oversensitive, hot-tempered, hyperactive and whining children.[77]

When I think about it, I realize that my mother looks at me only when I ask her to—'Can you please look at me while I am talking to you?'—because her eyes are otherwise busy on apps, like Blinkist or Elevate[78], on her phone. She rolls her eyes and looks at me, waiting for me to finish quickly.

Phone games, like Candy Crush, and Facebook have become the soulmates of most parents, while their children wait in the queue for their attention. Distracted parents cultivate distracted children, because parents who fail to focus pass on the same pattern to their children.

I completely agree that we sleep with our phones and wake up with them. Our phones and video games offer a 'new high' that stimulates and entertains us. We seek *sensational rush*, *independence* and a place to *experiment*. Drugs, smoking and alcohol are believed to help us attain this SIN—sensation, independence and novelty.

Now, video games and social media use have started to fulfil the same need.

'Monitoring the future,' an annual US government-funded report[79], which measures teenager drug use, says that the use

---

[77]https://ifstudies.org/blog/technoference-how-technology-can-hurt-relationships

[78]Blinkist is an app that distils the key insights of bestselling non-fiction books into 15 minutes reads or audio files. Elevate is an app that improves mind power.

[79]https://www.nytimes.com/2017/03/13/health/teenagers-drugs-smartphones.html?_r=0

of drugs like marijuana, cocaine, hallucinogens, ecclesia has reduced among children aged 12 to 17.

Many experts feel that use of phones and video games could plausibly be the reason behind the decline in substance abuse among high school children.

Though there are no conclusive studies yet, there seems to be a correlation between the steady decline in use of drugs and increase in use of the Internet and phones amongst teens.

I completely agree that it is a mere substitution of one monster by another. Digital instruments are helping us stay away from drugs as we can sit in a corner, pretending to be busy in some game or chat while our friends smoke pot or get tipsy. But they are enticing us to get into behavioural addiction.

'Screen' addiction is impacting us personally, socially, physically and creatively. Haven't we all started spending more time with these gadgets than our family and friends? We talk less, we argue less and we do not break our silence after a fight because we have our phones to go to.

Our social interactions are 'forwarded' messages, Snapchat stories and 'likes' and 'comments' collected online. When we meet, we click more pictures than anything else. We intend to meet to make the next FB post or Snapchat story.

We remain glued to our phones throughout the day, we do not move enough. Our physical activity is declining.

All this is sapping our creativity because our minds are always engaged. They are never bored, never empty to feel the pangs of creativity.

Within the next decade, we will come full circle. We already have a 'demetricator', which hides all the metrics of our posts on Facebook.[80]

We would need rehabilitation from digital addiction, we will have spas for digital detox. We will join companies which will clearly state a 'no-email from 6.00 p.m. to 8.00 a.m' policy. While others would hop in their driverless cars to buy an alarm clock some years later, let us order it now before it's too late.[81]

If you do so and watch the sun rise, please do not click a picture. Just be there.

Parents suck digitally because they pay attention to our digital lifestyle while ignoring their own.

They shout at us from the other room to not watch videos or play online games while they are glued to their smartphones.

Parents are scared that we waste our time online. They worry for our safety. What they are missing out right now is the 'behavioural addiction' dangerously lurking in the lives of *all* of us.

They need to understand:

- Addiction of drugs and alcohol was not easy to hide but addiction to online gaming, shopping, viewing and chatting is easier to hide. Most of the parents do not acknowledge their own addictions when packages from online shopping keep getting delivered to their

---

[80]'People are carrying around a portable dopamine pump,' says David Greenfield, founder of The Centre for Internet and Technology Addiction; https://www.mother.ly/parenting/is-technology-the-new-drug-for-our-kids-generation

[81]https://moonparenting.wordpress.com/2017/08/18/lets-buy-alarm-clocks/

> doorsteps every day or they are busy reaching to the next level of their games while having guests for dinner.
>
> ♦ Parents need to realize that our digital life has no footprints that we can follow. Online hooks, like Instagram, Amazon, World of Warcraft and Netflix, are so well-designed for repetitive use in such simplified and inexpensive ways that we all can get addicted. Addictive technology is a part of the mainstream in a way no other addictive substance ever was. Addiction is a result of situation and environment.

Since it is a new gratifying experience for all of us, we all fall in its trap. You being older need to get your act together first. Many of my friends tell me that it is a normal sight to have all family members sitting together glued to their phones. As soon as one person questions it, the others respond, 'I only took my phone out since you all were already busy on your phones.'

Phones neither argue, nor make fun of you. They appreciate you for playing, buying, watching. Who would want to miss that?

Rather than blaming each other for being games junkies or shopping suckers, let us do these activities together for a stipulated time.

Rather than trying to control each other, how about being more transparent about our favourite online activities?

You know, we love to show what we watch, play, share and laugh at, provided the listeners don't get into a judgemental mode.

Steve Jobs, who is the biggest reason behind our love for devices, never allowed his children to use an iPad because he knew about the addictive ingredients used in making the product.

As adults, parents need to be responsible netizens to ensure that our environment is a balanced mix of physical and digital activities.

Your silent observation and strategic communication would see to it that we are responsible digital natives. Your 'customary control' mode won't work.

REASON 35

Hide and Deny

Two marketing professors, Naomi Mandal and Eric Johnson, studied the impact of persuasion on buyers who visited an online furniture site. They showed two different wallpapers on the site's landing page to two different groups of visitors.

To one group, they showed wallpapers with fluffy clouds, while the other group was shown pennies on the wallpaper. The group which was welcomed by fluffy clouds searched the site for more information about comfort and chose a more comfortable and costly sofa, while the other group, welcomed by pennies, searched the site for cost information and bought an inexpensive sofa.

Not only this, when they were told about how their search behaviour and buying preferences were influenced by the wallpaper, most of the participants refused to believe it.[82]

Although adults get influenced by things, events and people, they refuse to accept it.

My father's friend visited an admission counsellor who suggested his daughter to pursue undergraduate studies in India and not abroad. My father persuaded me with all his might to visit the same counsellor. Since he is reluctant to let me go abroad for higher studies, he liked this counsellor. When I told him that he was forcing me to visit the counsellor

---

[82]Robert Cialdini. 2016. *Pre-Suasion: A Revolutionary Way to Influence and Persuade.* New York: Simon & Schuster. pp. 37–38.

under the influence of his friend's advice, he denied vehemently: '*Arre*! I am telling you to visit him as he is regarded as one of the best counsellors.'

As parents, you always observe other parents, assess their actions and get influenced by them. But when we tell you that you bought a fitness band because your friend got one, you will flat out deny it.

Many parents *hide* social influence because they believe that getting influenced is bad. Since they do not want to see themselves in a negative light, they try hard to prove it to themselves and others that they are not under the influence of anyone.[83]

A mother will push her child into the swimming pool because her friend's child was in the school newsletter with a swimming medal around her neck. Yet, she would disagree to any influence on her decision. She would like to believe that she wants her child to swim because it is the best exercise and the ideal stress buster. Parents want to give brownie points to themselves each day for walking that extra mile for their children. They want to prove it to themselves that they independently take a lot of decisions to enrich the lives of their children.

Many parents *deny* social influence because they genuinely do not see themselves as getting influenced. '*I* sent him to a new class', '*I* connected her to the person who will help her write a resume', '*I* showed him the video of the ICSE topper', '*I* downloaded a new app to check his online history'. 'Nobody else is doing it, it occurred to *me.*'

You want us to believe that you are the master of all

---

[83]Introduction to *Invisible Influence*, p.1.

your decisions when we clearly know that you rush me to a taekwondo class as soon as my classmate joins it. You feed me more avocado and kale when your friends rave about it. Also, you are always anxious as you do not want to miss out on anything that others around you are doing for their children.

We get influenced by our peers a lot. My friend who is studying at a top Indian college recently told me how he has taken to drinking alcohol due to extreme peer pressure. Our mothers were also in the room while we were having this conversation. My mom instantly told him that he should not be trying to fit in so much. '*Aur kya*, that's what I keep telling him,' chimed his mother. The next sentence from my friend, directed towards his mother, stumped me. 'You superficially agree with all the statements of grandmom and then say at the end, "*Karna padta hai* (You have to do it)". Dad entertains his clients even when he gets bored to death and says at the end, "*Karna padta hai*". Then where is the problem when I say, "*Karna padta hai*"?'

The CEO of a dog food company would eat the company's product (dog food!) at every annual shareholders meeting to convince people about its quality.[84] Brand endorsers try to do the same. It must be working, why else would a jewellery brand pay Salman Khan to be their ambassador![85] My mom's friend made her buy many protein powders and tablets when she joined a wellness brand. Mom, in turn, tried to give it to all of us. All the shakes and tablets landed in the dustbin after a year.

When you do things out of social pressure that you are

---

[84] https://www.ted.com/talks/adam_alter_why_our_screens_make_us_less_happy/transcript?language=en
[85] Salman Khan endorses PNG Jewellers.

conditioned to feel, I start feeling the same. I wish to get less influenced by other minds, including yours. How about trying it out with me? Let us be wary of the small nuggets of influence that are invisible to our eyes but invade our brains.

Parents' decisions get influenced by the actions of their peers, friends and relatives in both directions. They do exactly what their friends do. They do exactly opposite of what their friends do.

A friend told me that his father wanted to buy a specific car for the longest time. He would praise the car, research about it, read reviews online and was about to book it. Suddenly, he started condemning that brand and decided to buy some other car. His father's behaviour change puzzled my friend, till one day he came to know that his father's best friend had bought the same car. He did not want to buy something already bought by his friend. 'They are worse than children, dude,' said my friend.

A respondent wrote to me about an argument she had with her mother. 'While planning for a small get together at home, we were discussing the guest list. When I mentioned the name of a very dear friend of my mother, she told me not to include her as she was not in the city. I bumped into that friend incidentally and mentioned to her that we would miss her. She said that she was not going anywhere. Dumbfounded, my friend confronted her mother.

'I introduced her to X. They met each other through me. Nowadays, both of them hang out together without me. If she wants to be X's friend and not mine, it is fine with me!'

'Come on Mom! You all can be friends. By the way, how did you know that they 'hang' out together?'

'They posted pictures on FB. If she wants to be friend with X, I don't want to be her friend.'

Are these parents serious? If their friend becomes friendly with someone they knew from before, they get angry. The friend's action influences their friendship preferences.

Do you guys realize the lessons that you are passing on to us? Should I not buy a car of my choice because my friend has already bought it? Why should my choice depend on his?

Should I change my friendship with a person because she became friends with someone I introduced her to?
Since you hide such influences, it shows that they are not right. How about having a 'self-belief' and sticking to it?

How about encouraging us to stay away from peer influence rather than falling prey to it yourself? Rather than playing a game of 'hide and deny', how about transitioning to a game of 'acknowledge and avoid'?

REASON 36

We Live in Constant Summer

That's how parents feel. There is no spring when you raise children. As much as you feel tired by our constant clinging to you, you feel much worse when we stop clinging. As we grow up vertically, our peer group expands, our aspirations start occupying a lot of space in our heads and our attention shifts. We never knew that you did not know about it. We thought that you must have been there, done that. So, you would understand.

But you sulk silently. Moms who were the epicentre of our universe, do not want to give away the powerful position. Your abundant, but possessive, love feels threatened when new relationships brew. It shakes you up more than it should.

All parents love two things to be true forever:

- Our children are the centre of our lives. (They go to many lengths to prove it and they repeat it on a daily basis.)
- We are the centre of our children's lives. (Thanks to Lord Ganesha for circling around his parents when told to take a round of the world and raising the bar so high for us!)[86]

---

[86] Lord Ganesha and his brother, Kartikeya, were told to compete for a mango. Whosoever traversed the whole world first would get the fruit. Kartikeya immediately set off for his sojourn, while Ganesha simply took a round around his parents sitting on Mount Kailash. 'This is my world and I have travelled the whole world by moving around them,' he said.

They keep the 'control' button clenched in their fists. Homemaker moms want to stay useful around their kids. Even when the child learns to tie his shoe laces, she will continue to feed him from her hands ('He doesn't eat enough veggies otherwise,' is the plea). When he learns to lick everything off his plate, she will drive him to classes and help him with homework. When his 'self-study' and 'group study' scenes say goodbye to mothers, they begin looking for other matters to exercise their control.

The handing over of the baton doesn't come easy to most of the parents because of their over involvement in our lives. Lava-like tears flow out of their eyes with piercing verbal outbursts when they realize their children are not Lord Ganesha.

The protocol of 'asking' cannot easily move towards 'informing' parents. The movement from 'asking' to 'informing' causes a big control shift for which parents are never ready. Transformation from 'controlling decision-makers' to 'enabling liberators' is a dream for most children, even in adulthood.

Obedient children are liked more than competent children. Competence is celebrated publicly, but moaned privately because it brings independence and originality. Parents feel redundant and obsolete when the children take complete charge of their lives.

Children assist parents for so long in feeling 'in charge' that they consider themselves to be controlling far more than what they actually do. They wear the 'influencer' hat and flaunt it very often. Parents create an 'illusion of control' by offering incessant advice and unwarranted reprimands.

However, a daily dose of verbal and emotional instructions has an opposite effect. They blend in rather than stand out. Give me a playground and freedom to play. Please control your enthusiasm to check the best players, best techniques to play and best coaches. Please refrain from trying to make an impact.

Just as you have an undying love for your children, I have this unique connect with you where every journey would finally get me home. I want to travel the world with the conviction that I can go back home to my epicentre any time. My trust in you will never waver if you feel secure as a parent. A friend's mother once said, 'I can never lose my children. Wherever they live, whatever they do, my heart's key can find them.'

You are my safety net and that is why I want to try every adventurous free fall.

I heard another mother sulk the other day, 'Being a mother is the most thankless job.' It tore my heart. Do I need to thank my eyes every day for seeing everything? Do I need to thank my legs each time they carry me? I belong to you, I am a part of you. Don't you get it? I surely wish to spread my wings, fly high to explore new skies, but your thoughts, your words, your actions, your habits are an inseparable part of me. They make me who I am.

In 2016, Indra Nooyi wrote letters to parents of 4,000 senior executives at Pepsi Inc, thanking them for raising such amazing children who became such valuable employees. She received loads of loving replies from hundreds of parents leading to an amazing relationship development.

If your thoughts and habits did any good to me, then wait for that letter from my boss that s/he will write to you for giving them a valuable being like me. When I will scale new heights, people will come and congratulate you and shower you with attention. Though you don't need it, it could be a validation that you waited for.

I might not be saying thank you enough, I might not be

realizing your importance at the moment, I might be taking you both for granted (you did that to your parents too!), but I am grateful for having you.

Wait, I am grateful to you for having me.

Your journey with me is a journey in the fog, not on a railway track. Rather than a 'micro control' and 'micro manage' mindset, it will be relaxing and rewarding if we get 'freedom within framework' to begin and then 'freedom to design frameworks'.

Is it essential for you to spell out all the goals? How about letting them remain a bit fuzzy? Give us a canvas and colours but do not draw your preferred sketch, showing off the freedom that you hand over to us to paint it.

Sometimes, I might use the colours on a wall or chuck colours for charcoal.

REASON 37

I Love My Guilt

I work as a photographer on weekends with my Mom. So, I attend many of her leadership workshops and knowledge-sharing sessions. During one such session, I heard a mother, who was a doctor, talk about how her sudden and untimely work related calls made her guilty. She looked as if she was confessing to a crime. Her face emitted such shame and helplessness that my camera would have cried.

During the same session, a father shared the tale of his time constraints. He talked about his busy schedule with pride. He looked like a passionate salesman displaying his best product. His face emitted happy helplessness, that kind which is expressed by famous people when they cannot walk on crowded streets and have vada-pav.

Parents love their piece of the guilt pie. They vie for it. Their guilt comes in so many different shapes and sizes that each type of parent can have a DIY guilt trip package.

'I feel guilty because I worked so hard that I could not give enough attention to my children.'

'I feel guilty because I over supported them and crippled their independence.'

'I am guilty of being over indulgent.'

'I am guilty of being harsh and abusive.'

'I am guilty of expecting too much.'

I am guilty of expecting too little.'

Parents experience guilt because:

- **It is programmed in their 'perfect parent' identity.** A mother is expected to have all the time that a child deserves. She feels guilty because she is supposed to feel so when her work takes up the children's time.

    A father is expected to be very busy because he earns the money by remaining busy. He doesn't feel guilty when he doesn't have enough time. He would have felt guilty had he not earned enough according to the perfect parent identity.
- **Parents feel guilty because bandwagon bias influences them.** They weigh their behaviours and actions against others in their groups. Guilt keeps itching them as they compare themselves with others and scratch further—'X's mother travels with her for every sketching competition', 'Y's father got the school event sponsored'.
- **Parents suffer alone.** They don't share their guilt pangs easily with others if they face fear of being judged. Even when they have gone wrong, acknowledging it needs a giant heart. We wait for that acknowledgement which never comes.

Parents go on the guilt trip quite late, when their nests become empty or when they cuddle with their grandchildren.

Their guilt is often offered with a lot of pride and excuses. Pride, when they over protected, over advised and over stressed. Excuses, when they cared less, shared less or dared less.

Parents think that children should forget about their unacceptable behaviour once they acknowledge their guilt.

'Don't remind me of how rude I was with you. Don't bring

it up again and again. I am already guilty,' is the feeling of the parent.

Parents want to use their guilt acknowledgement as an eraser of the past. They wish their children should forget the hurt and be proud of their parents who have inflicted pain on themselves by admitting guilt.

It is like Kangana Ranaut exonerating Rajkumar Rao in the movie *Queen* because 'he apologized and showed remorse on abandoning her a day before their wedding.[87]

As parents, you personalize the guilt. You repetitively hold yourself responsible for anything that goes wrong in our lives. You emit guilt if I fall sick or misbehave, or when I perform the blasphemous act of underperforming.

Why do you feel that I am all because of you? It is not true. Period.

As parents, you make your guilt and grief all pervasive. You let it seep into all spheres of your lives: 'Since my child underperformed, I can't concentrate on my work', 'As he picked up a fight at school, how do I meet my friends and family who have such ideal kids?'

Why can't you compartmentalize? How about letting the guilt solidify than liquefy? No, wait. Solidified guilt will also do no good apart from making you feel heavy. Cancel the guilt trip and travel light rather.

You all feel guilty a tad too late. When the curtain goes

---

[87]*Queen*, a 2014 Indian comedy-drama, is about the nuanced self-discovery of a North Indian girl.

down on your active parenting days, you put your legs up, slide down in your armchair and look back. When you do so, you start feeling that you didn't play enough with your kids, you did not show your love enough, you did not take enough vacations. But this guilt cannot improve the situation. When the complete parent–child drama is playing out, you are too engrossed in making us feel guilty for every missed bus, bunked class and uncensored post. Rather than sulking permanently and pervasively, let's look for timely solutions.

How about feeling the guilt at the right time? When we are children, feel guilty for not spending enough time with us, for not encouraging us enough. Feeling guilty later is like thinking of repaying the debt to a person who is already dead. It serves no purpose.

Since you guys expect a lot from your parent position, you feel inadequate at any lapse. How about expecting less and accepting more?

Since group think influences you, guilt becomes a by-product of excessive and exaggerated information about others.

How about revoking the 'Herd Parent' in you?

Please accept your errors and admit them openly so that the guilt doesn't chew you up.

REASON 38

You Are in a Relationship with Your Amygdala

The daughter of a family friend got shortlisted for the audition of a musical reality show. The friend called my mother and shared the news.

'What about your daughter?' she asked.

'Umm...nothing...all is well with her, I guess.'

'No, no! She is a trained singer. Why doesn't she participate in such shows?' she pried, suggested, and interrogated.

'It doesn't interest her.'

'Oh! Anyway, please watch this show when my daughter comes on television.'

The euphoric telephone conversation sprayed excitement in the room.

Unfortunately, the daughter could not clear the audition and the mother was inconsolable and vitriolic.

Throughout this excessively emotional episode, I was thinking about the girl who would have experienced it all first-hand. She genuinely did not deserve to go through it. Why do you guys make it such a big deal when it is no deal?

Parents give immediate and overwhelming responses to real and imaginary actions of their children because they are in a permanent relationship with their amygdala. Amygdala is like the glasses that we use while watching a 4D film—everything appears closer and magnified. It heightens our senses.

Parents experience an extra dose of fear, anger, sadness,

loneliness and, of course, happiness for everything even remotely linked with their children.

Whatever I did, I did it for your good.

I sacrificed my dreams, my wishes to give you the best.

These are the 'E' bombs hurled at us, non-stop.

Ahem, Ahem!

You forced me to study commerce. It did good—to my tutors.

You enrolled me for swimming classes. It satisfied you—but terrified me.

You bought me Bose headphones—when I asked for ones by Beats.

You spent more on the headphones that you bought and termed them the best. You are so emotional about even headphones.

When we get emotional, we are ungrateful and complaining. When you get emotional (which is as frequent as WhatsApp notifications), you resemble a warrior wronged by his own men.

Different personalities of parents and different temperaments of children at various phases of their childhood get into the melting pot of life to create a volatile and vulnerable mosaic of emotions. Concoction of tears and tantrums, jugalbandi of hugs and high fives go hand in hand.

Earlier, my whining would drive my Mom crazy. Now, her involvement drives me nuts.

Parents take most of the decisions related to us based on either *whims* or *emotions*.

A whim is a person's desire, whose cause they don't know or care to know.

My mom told me to wear a particular dress the other day. When I asked the reason for it, she said, 'Because I want you to.'

My friend's mom is a doctor who runs her clinic in the evenings. My friend's grandmother told her mom one day, 'Don't come home so late.'

'Why?'

'Because I don't like it!'

How whimsical!

An emotion is an intense mental state which is subjective.

Ask some mothers to choose between these options:

You get a ₹50 card. You can either keep ₹20 or gain/lose it all.

You get a ₹50 card. You either gain/lose it all or lose ₹30.

If you pay attention, you would notice that they are economically equivalent. But they are not emotionally equivalent, says Daniel Kahneman. I am pretty sure that moms, who are emotionally aversive to the word 'loss', would immediately choose the first option. You guys always love safety and certainty, no matter how irrational it is. You love sure outcomes not because they are good for us but because they are good for you—they give you less stress than what uncertain outcomes would give.

Your animated faces turn babies as young as 2 months old into expert emotion readers. Within two months, they start grasping a happy face, a frowning face, an angry face or a fearful face. Not only this, infants start using the facial expressions of their caregivers as their gateways to the world.[88]

Before taking any action, they look back to their moms. A fearful face stops them while a smiling face signals them to march on. You wholeheartedly use these 'hot and cold' 'E' bombs in front of our friends.

---

[88] http://psychology.jrank.org/pages/212/Emotional-Development.html

You Are in a Relationship with Your Amygdala

As we grow up, we believe in the same social referencing but you start using your other face—a stiff face to disapprove almost everything that we do or propose to do. It is so difficult to break through a fenced face. An impervious rock looks softer in comparison to the stiff face which parents use whenever they want children to bow down, relent and abort all arguments. Showing no emotion is the new 'E' bomb.

But your stiff face breaks us into pieces and you know that. That's why you use it more frequently with our growing restlessness. The more we push you for uncomfortable answers, the more of your stiff face we get. Stiffness is the answer to all disturbing debates and dangerous fallouts.

Do we deserve this hardening of emotions for being our own person, for holding on to our own beliefs, for being who we are?

My cousin studies in a residential institute and keeps sharing the terrible and terrific tales of college-hood. He recently cut my call saying, 'Mummy calling. Bye.' His hurried goodbye was odd.

He called back after half an hour.

'The biggest crime in college is to miss your mother's call. Miss your extra class, miss your dinner but dare you miss your mom's call,' he shared his philosophy.

'You are funny,' I said.

'No, I am experienced,' he continued, 'I committed this crime last week. Mom called and my phone was in the pocket. I saw the missed call late. So, I called back the next morning. Then, I missed my breakfast.'

'Why?'

'*Arre*...she got terribly upset. Her tone was full of pathos—"No...it's ok...I will not call you every day."

"'No, Mum, I...'"
"'You are so busy. Why should I disturb you?'"
"*Aisa kuch nahi hai* (It's not like that)...'"
"'No, no, it's fine. You have forgotten your mom now.'"
"'Where are you going with this?'"
"'See, you are shouting now. You don't need to speak to me anymore. I keep worrying for you, but you have no attachment.'"

'My friends were calling me for breakfast.'

"'Aa raha hoon, yaar!" I said in irritation.'

"'Go, go, enjoy.'"

"'They are calling me for breakfast.'"

"'You go na!'"

'The tone made me feel like a criminal.'

I was laughing at his narration.

'You don't become a criminal like me when you go to college.'

'Yes boss!' I said in jest.

'Amygdala in action' causes elders to feel non-existent fears and surreptitious sadness. It makes them rude, and nasty too.

Researchers Barry Staw, Katy DeCelles and Peter Degoey studied 305 half-time locker room speeches by coaches of twenty-three school and college basketball teams. Many coaches had the most boisterous outburst, full of anger, verbal abuse and even throwing things. Research suggested that performance of teams whose coaches were repulsively rude went downhill after half time.

Rudeness by coaches, seniors and parents causes either fearful shame or reciprocal rudeness.[89]

---

[89]Robert I. Sutton. *The Asshole Survival Guide: How to Deal with People Who Treat You Like Dirt.* p. 28.

We catch 'emotions' like 'cold'. If parents are happy, children tend to be stress-free and happy. When parents are stressed and frustrated, kids tend to feel the same.

Indian parents are platinum members of the 'emotions club'. All the negative and positive emotions flow freely and 'abundantly'.

How about taming your emotions? As parents, the best survival strategy is to be stoic.[90]

Your emotional expressions of tears, sadness, loneliness and pain stress us. How about judging the events from an honest lens? It is not the event that makes you emotional, but your belief about the event. How about interpreting your feelings wisely?

Your emotional expressions of anger, frustration, control and threat intimidate us. How about learning to 'let go' completely?

No one can actually control the other person or most of the situations. How about being realistic?

---

[90]There are two fundamental principles of stoicism: (i) People are not disturbed by events but by their interpretations of the events; and (ii) It is critical to know what we can control and what we can't.

REASON 39

The 'What If' Buzzer

I don't remember this because it happened a day after my first birthday but it pops in our family conversations often.

After a big bash for my parents (how can the first birthday celebration be a celebration for me?) the previous night, my mother needed some time to rearrange the house full of gifts. My father was assigned to the task of looking after me for some time. He took me out, lifted me up to the front wall and let me stand on it with my wobbly feet, while holding both my hands.

He was reciting or singing something but a barking dog on the road caught my fancy. I turned around, let his hand go and lost my balance. There I went like a free-falling Frisbee towards the ground.

I remained lying on the ground, while my father stood frozen next to me. My mother heard the fall and came out running. She scooped me from the ground while shooting questions at my father. Meanwhile, I started wailing. My mother was shaken, but my father went so numb that he was unable to drive me to the doctor. My mom called up my grandfather (thank you Nana for staying so close), who then came and took us to the hospital. I survived the fall and I have been surviving the fears of my father since then.

Whenever I tell my Dad that he dropped me and then didn't even pick me up, he 'reasons', '*Arre*! I got so scared!'

Parents conceive a 'what if' buzzer in their brain the day they conceive us.

'Baby's day in' are marked with fears, like 'Is the growth fine?' 'Is every organ growing?' 'Is the baby kicking?' 'Is the baby kicking enough?'

'Baby's day out' starts a *fearful* tale. When you type 'Funny fears of parents' in Google, you end up taking a master class in 'how to discover fear in everything'.

Parents have fears, like 'My baby might drown in a toilet' or 'get crushed under me'.

Science says that humans can smell fear. I think parents can see, touch, taste, hear and, of course, smell fear, everywhere. They imagine fear. They create fear and gift it to everyone.

Parents suck because fear is their permanent companion. They are wrapped up in perpetual fear when we are newborns, as a human infant is far more helpless than the newborns of any other species.

Parents live in 'fear of now': They fear more about what will happen right now than what will happen a decade later. In their book, *Freakonomics*, Steven D. Levitt and Stephen J. Dubner tell us to imagine a government official, who is expected to procure funds for one of the two lethal problems—terrorist attacks and heart diseases. Though more people need help for heart diseases, politicians and philanthropists will easily offer help to fight terrorist attacks. Why? Because terrorist attacks happen now while death by heart disease is some distant catastrophe. Parents get terrified too easily and fail to judge the real risk factors.

Peter Sandman, at Princeton University, concluded that risks that scare people and risks that kill people are very different.[91] Parents, in their state of perpetual fear fail to assess risk properly and overreact when outrage is far more than an actual hazard. A death by a terrorist attack is much less likely but creates much more outrage as compared to a death by heart failure which is far more likely but will create much less outrage. So, parents will worry more about keeping their children safe from a terrorist attack than worrying about their healthy diet. They are more scared of a toddler crying on a shop floor for a chocolate than a teenager who always manipulates them by howling and non-stop shedding of tears.

The *Freakonomics* authors talk about a wonderful American phenomenon where a parent will never send his daughter to the house of a friend whose dad owns a gun, but will easily allow her to go to a friend's house which has a swimming pool.

Though more children die each year in swimming pool mishaps than shooting incidents, swimming pools do not inspire as much outrage as guns do. Hence, parents assess risks wrongly and do not take corrective measures. They need to be more careful around swimming pools which could easily save hundreds of children every year.

Rather than breathing fear, they need to think about safety measures of actual risks. Rather than being dramatic about dangers of terrorism, please rationally examine the dangers of a careless dive by your kid in a swimming pool.

'Being fearful' is an acquired skill for all the parents, so much so that they are at a loss when it comes to deciding when to use it.

My mom says: In the first decade of childhood, parents are scared for us. In the next, they are scared of us.

---

[91] Dubner and Levitt, *Freakonomics*, p. 136.

The first-decade fear fighting prayer is, 'I hope my child is safe.'

The second-decade fear fighting prayer is, 'I hope my child doesn't create trouble.'

'Fear of losing the child' is the fundamental fear that manifests itself in myriad ways. Parents suck because this perpetual panic mode makes them overbearing. A respondent wrote, 'My father is a rule Nazi. I am expected to finish my shower under ten minutes. If I don't step out in time, he worries that I might have died inside.' Phew!

Do you guys realize that your overbearance is diluting the 'collective intelligence' of our family by not letting us communicate clearly with you. When 'fear and control' do the talking, the family bond gets muted.

Fear makes you temperamental. You worry about kidnappings, but allow your children to ride bikes without helmets. You do not let us travel alone, but we walk through online alleys all the time.

Fear makes you insensitive tyrants, as you try to protect us from imaginary and real fears.

Do you guys realize that your fear of fear is contagious. It makes us doubt everything and stay in permanent anxiety.

It is perfectly fine to be alert and cautious but you guys exaggerate it.

How about teaching us to ride a bike with a helmet rather than making us ride pillion with you.

How about facing the fear rather than fearing it?

Verbalizing fear all the time is like chanting for mishaps.

Why do you wish to invite trouble? 'You care for us' is not the same as 'you fear for us'.

Facing our fears with confidence is the best gift a parent can give to his child.

REASON 40

Private Tutors, Surrogate Learning

Parents love outsourcing. They are infatuated with outsourcing—studies, projects, get togethers, food, hobbies, college applications and homework. You are the best talent-acquisition leaders, who search online for reviews and offline for friends to know about their experiences to hire tuition teachers, instructors, music teachers, career consultants and event managers.

Just as the earth revolves around the sun without fail, each child revolves around various experts out of school.

You feel so happy and relaxed when your child is all sorted with tuitions, hobby classes and other assistance. You connect them with the right set of experts and let loose your purse strings.

Rather than working on your own weaknesses in languages or Maths, you only hone your selection skills.

If you guys would have studied a few subjects with me when I was younger, we would have known the subjects, and each other, better. I would not have fooled you the way I fooled all the hired helps.

Since you outsourced 'your time' to a bandwagon of experts, I outsourced my brains to video games and PlayStations.

We craved to have more time with you while dabbling into new areas. We wanted to enjoy cricket, chess, singing, drawing, taekwondo, swimming, coding with you, because we wanted you to see what we were experiencing. Had you partnered with us in the starting years, we would have made a smoother bond with you. We know that you guys have your hands full, but then, we are not a new product, assembled and packaged by different mentors, decorated at the end with a 'Made by Parents' tag.

You are overwhelmed, tired and restless, so are the experts to whom you hand us over.

You spend more time with 'Candy Crush' than with me. Do you know, my tuition teachers and coaches are no different?

You are swimming in the digital deluge by being a professional available 24x7, which means that you are not mindfully and heartfully available to us.

A recent survey reveals that 87 per cent of primary school and 97 per cent of high school students in metros receive private tutoring.[92] The number of private tutors exceed the number of school teachers.

We go to school, obey the school teachers and do the homework.

We go to coaching classes, cram the tips and slog to meet deadlines.

We come home, get advised and conk out.

Your social obsession with private tutoring should be acknowledged by government bodies.

In fact, the coaching industry is now being called the surrogate mother of education. But, when a surrogate mother is on the job, the mother waits for the baby. They do not work simultaneously. Then why are we subjected to both simultaneously?

---

[92] http://www.dnaindia.com/academy/report-the-great-indian-tuition-and-coaching-industry-1973985

A study[93] reveals that one-fifth of the students who attend private tutoring do so because of parental decision. For parents, merely studying in schools is like putting together a quick meal at home; whereas, attending private tutoring is equal to preparing a gourmet dish in a renowned restaurant. Why do we need to prepare both meals? It is causing obesity and indigestion.

The study further states that sending children to prestigious coaching centres is a matter of social status for middle-class Indian parents. It makes them feel exclusive. The more money and guilt you have, the more coaching and hobby classes we go to.

My grandparents tell me that going to tuition classes was an embarrassment in their childhood and, now, not attending enough coaching classes is an embarrassment.

You guys are lazy and linear thinkers. You think lazily as you believe in the same archaic parenting principles which are obsolete now. You think linearly as you want us to take the same paths that you took.

I intend to design the new satellite for Tesla[94] while you dream for me to join ONGC (Oil and Natural Gas Corporation).

How about spotting the new trends rather than appreciating the old mantras?

You guys must know about the 'Big Fish-Little Pond Effect'. Psychologist Herbert Mersh, the propounder of this effect says:[95]

---

[93]https://ries.revues.org/3913

[94]Tesla is an American firm that specializes in electric vehicles, energy storage and solar power manufacturing. (Wikipedia)

[95]https://www.ncbi.nlm.nih.gov/pubmed/10508530; Malcom Gladwell has

- The school choice made by parents and children is based on wrong reasons. Each parent wants that his/her child should get into the best school/college.
- The more elite an educational institute is, the worse students feel about their own academic abilities. It is not a surprise to see that the top two students of a 'good' institute can become the 'bottom two' students of a 'really good' institute.
- What is better: To be known as Amitabh Bachchan of a city or to be known as Asrani of a nation? (Use Google if you haven't heard about famous artist Asrani.)
- The positive effects of elite schools are seen more imminently on the 'self-concept' of parents, rather than the children.
- Children might feel miserable at a top college while parents remain on the 'top of the world'.

Expecting excellence from your children is natural but excellence does not mean getting admitted to the highest ranked institute for everyone.

Satya Nadella, CEO of Microsoft, studied Electrical Engineering at Manipal Institute of Technology, and not at the topmost engineering college of India. There are plenty of people who graduate from the topmost institutes and are still not happy or satisfied. There are plenty from average institutes who feel successful and lead a life full of purpose.

---

also talked about this concept in his book, *David & Goliath*.

How about imbibing 'love for lifelong learning' in me rather than a 'distaste for learning'? Please do not think about the immediate and short-lived happiness that you will get when these tuitions and mechanized coaching classes thrust me into a top college somehow. Please observe my potential and temperament before getting fixated with my career in your head.

REASON 41

Rent a Car, Own a Ride

Parents are so busy preparing to have the last laugh that they don't even remember when they laughed last.

You guys think that you are on a very serious mission of making monsters morph into megastars. You stay in a 'red alert' mindset, keeping yourself and us on a leash. When you decide to loosen the leash for some downtime, you have your own ideas of having fun, which are 'tried and tested' by others.

We all have been on so many flights and have gone through equal number of in-flight security announcements made in the dreariest tones and most mundane ways possible. Well, parents are like these flight attendants who are duty-bound to carry out the operational procedures. How can they make in-flight security announcements less serious and more fun? If they do not play by the script, they might lose their jobs.

I took a Southwest airlines flight from New York to Chicago this summer and had such a memorable time.

The flight attendant started the security announcement with:

> 'Good morning on this hot, very hot morning. We welcome you all aboard. The seat pockets store, apart from dirty diapers, banana peels and used cans that you will leave for us, the security manual. Please don't stare at us, read it.

> There may be fifty ways to leave your lover.
> There are only eight ways to leave this plane.[96]

I laughed hard and Southwest airlines won another fan.

They created the most monotonous experience into a memorable one. For the first time, I listened to the safety instructions. How about making our routine have such defining moments?

Parents love scripts. They get scared even if we miss to follow any comma or full stop in the script. They see to it that we dot all our i's and cross all the t's while copying the blockbuster script.

Though they have started to inch towards making memories alongside making careers, these memories are also scripted through a group vacation customized by a tour operator.

It is fun to create moments that stay with us for a lifetime, but such moments can neither be designed nor anticipated. They just happen.

Parents, being preoccupied with prescriptions of living life, miss these moments that elevate our spirits for years to come. There are many moments of togetherness that can light up our relationship but we are so stuck in playing to the tune that no new rhythm reaches our heart.

It is the easiest to nurture a bond between you and us because so many ingredients of making a close-knit bond for life are inherently present. There is unexplainable emotional energy between us which gets eroded by lowly concerns of acing exams, winning championships and beating others hollow. How about using this emotional energy to multiply happiness, not fear?

---

[96] https://www.youtube.com/watch?v=TxNrizGdhtY

There is an undying trust between us which is corroded by the free-flowing fear of drunk driving, porn-watching and fooling others. How about using this trust to multiply faith, not suspicion?

Indian parents preserve everything from platinum bands to polythene bags. 'Preserve the Past' or 'Prepare for Future' is your mantra, while 'Living the Present' is ours. 'Buying your own home' or 'buying your own car' enslaved your youth while airbnb and Uber have liberated ours to collect experiences, not things. You had portfolio of investments, we wish to have a portfolio of careers.

Once you are done using the 'preserving the past' excuse, your urge to control the future takes over. You feel safe when you have plenty of money, material and machines in control.

Your 'Safe & Secure' is our 'Happening & Satisfying'. We neither preserve the past nor tame the future. We want to live the present and 'yolo' (You Only Live Once) is our anthem.

Parents slogged to educate their children, get them married in socially acceptable ways and build a retirement home. Every iota of energy was channelized to tick these boxes. We don't think like this.

Marriages should not be treated as gateways to splurge anymore because no one knows when we would need to pay the lawyer. Sitting at one place for all my life seems like a distant dream, so my wandering spirit will not get attached to one house.

We will save for the rainy day, but not hoard for the monsoon. You collected letters, preserved books, saved heirlooms, but we wish to travel light. We are fine with giving away things and cluttering only our hard disks.

We want to be safe, but unlike ships in a harbour. We want to make memories, but unlike ruminating cows. The 'Delete' button can be used to declutter and we hit it with detachment. Since technological advancement is forcing organizations to create 'fast history', attachment to strategies that worked yesterday will tamper with our today and destruct our tomorrow. Deconstructing and disrupting our minds by adapting to fast-paced change is a given for us. The dynamic of rising up and crumbling down is fast and welcome.

How about fastening your seat belts to enjoy our roller-coaster rides?

REASON 42

Role-self Mash-up

A good song mash-up has these qualities:

- Integration: It integrates distinct apps or songs for a wholesome experience.
- Distinction: Despite aggregation, the individuality of each app or song is not lost. The mere method of sequencing them creates a different experience.
- Originality versus creativity: The content here is not original but creatively pieced together, just like life.
- Fixation: Repeated exposure to something in a specific sequence creates a habit of getting fixated by the same order. Listeners or users get used to the specific rhythm.

Adults love role mash-ups. They integrate different professional and relationship roles and play them in a sequence. It is difficult to get out of the skin of one role and slide into another.

A man plays the role of a manager or doctor for eight to ten hours every day and then keeps coming in and out of other professional roles of being a team leader, a subordinate to his boss, chairing some social committee or engaging with some professional network.

Some adults successfully make the distinction between different roles and shuttle well, while some cannot. Adults thrive on 'authority' in their professional roles and use 'emotion' in their relationship roles.

Some of them stay in an authority mode round the clock,

appraising and supervising everyone while some stay in their patronizing mode, judging and protecting everyone.

An expert singer can quickly transition from the rhythm of one song to the next, but many would mix up and continue with the previous melody in the next song.

There are many mothers who want their children to report to them every day. There are leaders who behave like protective and critical parents most of the time.

Such mash-ups between various roles and between a role and the self create a mosaic of confusion for us who get our first experiences of roles through your behaviour.

A bossy father or an authoritarian mother makes us feel that this is what fathers and mothers should be like. My recordings of childhood get flawed for life. You not only falter in raising a child but also give wrong cues to a future father/mother that resides in me.

When parents cannot smoothly transition from one role to another by staying mindful, we get shocks and surprises. A frustrated employee at work forgets to switch off the dissatisfied mode when he reaches home and can turn family time into a battleground filled with negativity. An overprotective mother at home can approach every decision with the lens of fear at her workplace.

When you remain attached to your professional or social field of play, why can't we stay attached to our online and offline friend groups. I would love to stay in my 'abusing, binging, challenging, dabbing' avatar in front of you. When we bear the CEO or colonel or actor mode of yours, it would be fun to see us in our 'friends' mode.

It is so important to peel off the 'professional roles' to get into the 'relationship roles', finally reaching the 'self'. Fathers who remain CEOs at home or CEOs who remain mothers at workplace fail to make the required role swaps.

Since you are so busy playing various roles, fulfilling diverse expectations, the relationship with self takes a beating. Removing all make-up of expectations to welcome the sight of real self is a tomorrow that never comes.

You take all your roles so seriously that you do not discern between your roles and the real you.

When I disagree with you, have an argument with you, throw tantrums or get melodramatic, I am talking to the parent role of yours. You take it personally and feel disrespected and hurt.

Why do you take it personally when it is aimed at the parent in you, and not at you? I get angry with the mom role that you play, I fret and fume at the father role but I am fine with you.

The way we juggle from solving Maths problems to analysing in literature to testing science concepts, you need to juggle from the 'boss' at workplace to 'coordinator' at social meetings to 'parent' at home.

The way my 'self' chooses one subject over the other and signals me to drop the rest, you should listen to your 'self' before venturing into so many roles.

How about not being a parent if your heart does not wish to play the role?

How about not playing to the social gallery but connecting to your core before getting into life-altering roles?

Though you would remain my parents forever, it will be great to connect at the level of 'self' so that a mutual respect and understanding is developed to cement our bond for years after growing up.

Once I fit in your shoes, we need to create a new mash-up as individuals who love and respect each other, not by chance, but by choice. How about taking the pressure out and bringing participation in? How about replacing expectation with empathy?

Let us look forward to chuck the parent–child mash-up for a 'two collaborators' mash-up after we grow up enough.

The way your 'parent' role sometimes pushes you to get unjustifiably mad at us, my 'child' role sometimes takes my little common sense away. Then, I get aggressive beyond measure, I become touchy beyond control and I become a nightmare. You should not get completely consumed by the parent in you, and the child in me should not overtake my responsibilities as a student or a musician.

Our mash-ups are too intense to handle at times. How about refraining from parent-zoning all your roles?

How about going for a detox vacation to nourish your 'self' without waking up the parent in you? How about making a smooth and quick swap from the professional in you to the parent in you to the person in you?

REASON 43

Blue and Pink

I love photography more than most of the things I do. My classmates were producing the first school feature film as a project. Owing to my passion and some work experience, I interviewed for the position of the cinematographer. The supervisor was excited to have me on board, but the boys were not sure.

Throughout the making and launching of the film, I felt challenged. The technical crew did not like to take instructions from me. They questioned my competence on outdoor shoots and were downright rude and nasty. I was laughed at, I was ignored. I was coerced to agree to their way of doing things. It made me think about what lessons we were learning as teenage boys and girls.

When I spoke to my mother, she told me about the #LikeaGirl Campaign[97] and also the Bechdel Test[98].

The campaign made me understand how the stereotypes inherited by families and societies collectively impact the psyche of girls at puberty.

The test made me realize how our films were deepening

---

[97] https://www.youtube.com/watch?v=XjJQBjWYDTs&t=93s

[98] Bechdel Test is a way of evaluating whether or not a film or other work of fiction portrays women in a way that is sexist or characterized by gender stereotyping. To pass the test, a work must feature at least two women, who must talk to each other, and their conversation must concern something other than a man.

the gender stereotypes. It judges a film by asking three simple questions to assess the female presence, influence and involvement in the film.

The three questions are:

- Are there at least two women playing important characters?
- Do they talk to each other?
- Do they talk about something other than a man?

The film that I shot, incidentally, failed the test miserably, like most of the films.

It is not about the girls alone. It is equally about the boys. Parents stereotype both. Elders, teachers, media, professional scenarios deepen it further.

Had Jude Brady[99] written about sons and daughters, it would have, perhaps, read like this:

I want a daughter who is pretty like a princess. I want a son who is macho like a superhero.

I want a daughter who is nice to everyone. I want a son who is tough with everyone.

I want a daughter who shows respect to me and fears me without showing it to the world.

I want a son who at least shows respect in front of the world.

An ever-agreeing, artistic daughter is welcome. An ever-challenging, athletic son is welcome.

---

[99] http://www.columbia.edu/~sss31/rainbow/wife.html; Do read the famous 'I Want a Wife' essay by feminist and activist Judy Brady to fully understand my thoughts.

> *I want a daughter to be grateful as I want one. I want a son to be as he is wanted.*
>
> *I want a daughter to be a wife. I want a son to be a winner.*

Many parents will not agree at first that they are bullied by their biases; but please, dig deeper to pick the hidden patterns. A boy can't cry and a girl can't be aggressive; a boy can't give up and a girl can't hold on—you all say and believe in such stereotypes.

More skin lightening creams are sold in South Asia than bottles of Coca-Cola.[100] 'Abuse' is like that Vodafone pug for girls—it follows us everywhere. The number of working women in our country is shrinking in the same way our memory for remembering tables/phone number is. We study longer but then decide to let it all fizzle out because our family thinks we are a better value-add inside the home.

Though I am a teenager with some brain development still pending (neurology says so!), I fail to understand the definition of 'work'.

I see all these mothers at parent–teacher meets (PTMs), school events and various workshops conducted by my mother who tell each other: 'I am not working right now…growing kids, ailing parents, very busy husband…I can't work'. So, raising children, looking after parents, managing household is not work.

Well, mothers think so. Fathers definitely think so. Then, it must be right.

Women are expected to prove that they are working and

---

[100] http://news.bbc.co.uk/2/hi/8546183.stm

contributing. Women also try to prove it all the time because their value addition generally does not bring money in the bank account.

Mothers get judged for how they maintain the household, how well we behave, how well we score, but fathers can't be judged at home because they do not do this menial stuff. They bring in the moolah which is the most important task (because fathers do it!) and, hence, the patriarchy expects us to be more grateful and respectful to the fathers, grandfathers and the male relatives.

In respectful universities of India, different rules exist for girls and boys. There are places where girls are not allowed to use phones after 10 p.m. in their hostel rooms while boys can. Girls are not allowed to have non-vegetarian food while boys can.[101] These universities are real, honest universities because they are keeping up the flag that families have hoisted in their homes.

The domestic distinction between girls and boys, vibrantly visible at homes, becomes a rule book in such institutions. What parents start is rightfully carried forward by institutions of all types.

Freedom of choice is a malware and parents function as anti-virus software for us.

We are not born with free will, because, first, we are children and more important, we are daughters.

We do not 'have' freedom. We are 'allowed' freedom.

Is it only our 'physical safety' that worries our parents? If that is so, train us to kick rather than cook.

Is it our dreams and desires that scare your socially secure

---

[101] http://www.livelaw.in/gender-discriminatory-hostel-rules-bhu-sc-lens/

stature? If that is so, train your *'Log kya kahenge?'* (What will the people say?) page to hit *refresh*.

I am blessed as I am an only child. I am kind of more blessed because my mom doesn't have a brother. So, she is 'gender bias' challenged in the same way as she is 'remote control' challenged.

But, it is in the air. You breathe it. It is a deeply held belief, a fiercely protected family recipe in most of the households. Many parents cherry-pick sons in the womb. You guys suck because you prefer one gender over the other. It is a slot machine game—try, kill, try, kill until you get a boy.

Research suggests that if counter views and facts are offered to change or correct deeply held beliefs, the person begins to feel more strongly about those beliefs. If I believe in this 'Backfire effect'. What solution do I have for trying to turn parents gender neutral?

Kristina Durante from Rutgers Business School, through a study across the US and India[102] concludes that parents subconsciously spend more money on the child of the same gender as themselves but are clueless about it. When fathers are the financial decision-makers in a family and they identify more with their sons, daughters become disadvantaged automatically.

Also, it is very difficult to reason somebody out of a position or a belief that they didn't reason themselves into, says Daniel J. Levitin in his book, *Weaponized Lies*[103]. It is difficult to change the beliefs that are based on emotions and not rational thought.

---

[102]http://epaperbeta.timesofindia.com/Article.aspx?eid=31804&articlexml =Mothers-spend-more-on-their-daughters-than-fathers-05102017116013

[103]Daniel J. Levitin. 2016. *Weaponized Truth: How to think critically in the post-truth era*. New York: Dutton.

You guys fuel your emotions and then fool ours. Parents have made up their minds emotionally about their children, especially girls, regarding how they should think, talk, sit, decide(?); what they should eat, study, watch, read, wear; when they should smile, cry, comment, marry, have children, leave their jobs, compromise, adjust; and why they should be happy, grateful, hard-working, flexible, attractive and sympathetic.

Today's parents are making the same emotional errors that our grandparents made.

They worked on their daughters and left their sons to come home, throw their shoes and clutch the TV remote.

These sons, who are our fathers now, are passing on almost similar lessons to their sons, who will start similar family stories with us with plots like:

- Girls top in schools and colleges and get toppled over in life.
- Girls do menial, mundane, repetitive work that is ignorable while boys work on life-altering projects.
- 24x7 moms are ticking time bombs and weekend moms are selfish.
- 'Limited edition' dads or ATM dads are the norm.

How about making our families to write new stories, such as:

- Everyone should 'live' life in schools and thereafter too, topping or no topping.
- Work has no gender. Daily chores are important and boring. Divide the boredom to multiply pleasure.
- Families are the safest places to be oneself.
- Family vision, collectively written by all, should be the norm.

Just like parents of yesterday, parents of today expect daughters to adapt, adjust and accommodate more than the sons. They expect sons to be alpha males who are protectors, wealth creators and decision-makers.

Professor Christopher F. Chabris says the teams that have at least a few women are smarter than those which have no women at all.

If a family is a team, it generally has women on board, but their intelligence might not be getting utilized the way it should be.

Parents do a major disservice to their 'family smarts' when they discount or decide to ignore the power of a female mind.

Research suggests clearly that women are socially more intelligent and can raise the team work to a new level.

When a husband thinks that his professional problems are complex and his wife can handle simpler domestic issues only, he ignores two realities. First, domestic issues are deeper and graver. Second, a woman's perspective can simplify his professional problems. (She might be helping others solve their problems online while you are battling out alone.)

'Domestic disregard' of a girl and a woman will rock our family boats completely if parents of today do not decide to re-engineer their gender prejudices.

'Mask of Masculinity' on every boy's face will destroy our families if parents of today do not let boys be vulnerable and emotional.

If a father fails to equalize the domestic equation, his son and daughter will imbibe the inequality and ruin the future families too.

If a mother fails to see and wipe her son's tears, her children will end up raising fake families.

You guys can begin the biggest social innovation in your families.

I don't know what we are waiting for!

REASON 44

Love Means Zero

In their podcast 'Question of the Day', Steve Dubner and James Altucher posed a question: 'When is cursing appropriate?'[104]

Sharing one of his memorable experiences, Dubner recollected a family vacation where he was strolling on a quaint New York Road behind a church along with his wife and children. The road was quiet and empty. As the family strolled silently, they suddenly heard a loud voice, 'What's up Motherf***?'

They turned around. It seemed like someone called out to them. What they saw was a young boy, leisurely talking over the phone.

They laughed heartily and Dubner's daughter suggested to go after him to find what all he was saying.

It became a bonding moment for the family, so much so that Dubner confided to using the phrase every morning with his children.

It set a smiling and shared tone to the tune of their day.

The way we use words indicate our cultural vibrancy and personal gravitas.

As individuals, you love to construct an emotional mosaic of words by piecing together abuses, swears, curses and doublespeak. As parents, you tend to hide behind euphemisms to shift gears to take a responsible and rational position. As parents, you are hypocritical users of language.

---

[104]http://freakonomics.com/question-of-the-day-podcast/, episode 55

When we are young, rather than talking normally to us, you show your love by baby talk—talking to us like a toddler. It is we who are new at the speaking business, not you. Why do you talk to us as if you have lost your original sounds and pronunciations?

We listen to your animated voices and then face the real world and get confused. We will pick up the right words with correct pronunciation far quickly if you avoid your baby talk. And when we get used to your childish manner, you try to talk us out of it. It seems you do this theatrical hyper-articulation to enjoy our innocence and cuteness factor which lasts only for the first few years. As we grow up, it becomes an annoyance for you. But for us, it is an upheaval. We do not see the changes in us. We feel the same needs. You force us to change. When you wanted us to eventually become like you, why did you give us false hopes in the first place by baby talking?

Profanity is banned in ideal and formal circumstances, but it is viral in all informal settings (we know that!). Sometimes, cuss words are a sign of intimacy in friendships, authority in relationships and chutzpah in perceptions. You use them frequently in our absence and bite your lip when you miss our presence while stringing abuses in your sentences.

We use it with our friends (you know that!). We use it as a social accessory to show off our 'coolness' quotient. My friends idolize those new stand-up heroes who are certainly witty, but swear profusely to show that they are one of us (or to prove that we are one of them!).

You cuss and so do we, but with a curtain in between. You feign ignorance and stick to your belief that your children do not use swear words.

Even when you swear in a cool and reckless manner in our

absence, it reaches us somehow and we emulate you. Adults who swear with panache infect so many youngsters with it—more with the style they use it, less with the word itself. When I was younger, I heard so many cuss words from my friends who must have heard them while commuting or talking to seniors or peers or at home.

The angrier we are, the more we swear. Angry parents say things that hurt forever. Such language outbursts are common and catastrophic. The headmistress of a school in Glasgow banned parents from entering the compound at the end of the day as many parents were using offensive language with the staff. She passed a notice to the parents to stay in designated zones and not indulge in shouting and using abusive language which was being witnessed by the pupils too.[105]

Every adult swears somewhere or the other but generally maintains restraint in front of his/her children. The way we pick other words from whatever we hear around us, swearing also enters our word collection from some medium—TV shows, school friends, adults or, maybe, you. Though you try really hard to bulletproof us from profanity, it leaks in from some hole.

You do not want us to swear for two reasons. First, any swearing child is considered to be undisciplined and aggressive. Our social conditioning declares him to be a child of permissive parents who are low on values.

Second, you do not want your children to use it in front of you at least. Though you fail sometimes to control your urge to blurt out an 'F' bomb in front of us, we need to be the epitome of courtesy and politeness. Believe me, we have

---

[105]http://www.telegraph.co.uk/education/2017/02/07/parents-banned-talking-teachers-school-gate-following-claims/

this great rush to follow you in your absence and we fulfil this urge as soon as we get an opportunity.

Parents love 'euphemisms', the politically correct ambush to soften every blow. Euphemisms shelter us from the reality but sometimes lean towards incorrect cultural conditioning. Menstruating becomes a 'girl's problem' and, hence, is not to be spoken about openly like shaving.

Three areas where you are conditioned to use euphemisms are: genitalia, sex and death. You guys try to replace a penis or vagina with wee wee. Would you call a hand a 'hee hee'? Why do you want us to give special attention to some organs?

For how long do we want to fool ourselves by hiding our obsession for hypocrisy? Your sons and daughters, who inhabit this world somewhere with me, think and fantasize about these organs as unreachable conquests that they would reach some day.

When you use euphemisms, we learn the tricks of the trade before learning the trade. You don't know what we mean when we say things like 'scooping' or 'doing laundry'.[106]

We are actually beating you at your own game of using euphemisms.

But your euphemisms can get dangerous when they disassociate us from the ground reality.

I fail at an exam or a tournament and you tell everyone, 'S/he appeared in it only for gaining experience. Her goal is to make it next year.'

My friend enrolled for a swimming class but her dad pleaded, 'I am scared of water and I love you too much to

---

[106]Scooping means to make a sexual advance; Doing Laundry means having sex; https://www.urbandictionary.com/define.php?term=laundry

let you get into the water every day.' Later, he revealed that he did not want her skin tone to get darker due to swimming. This puffery is an exaggeration of your intention and opinion.

Though we understand that we need the support of some euphemisms about sex-related curiosity, it needs answers without raised eyebrows and embarrassed, hushed tones.

'Where do babies come from?' can't be addressed with a biological explanation at 5 years of age, but it cannot be laughed at. If you won't tell us, Uncle Google will. It is fine to use euphemisms around death till we get friendly with the idea of its inevitability. From then on, it can be faced with a more realistic expression.

When we are reminded again and again not to use these words, we understand their power.

For many, swearing is like yawning. Research suggests that the more we are sheltered from these words, the more impressive they become.[107] Though nobody wants us to use them, we do. Sometimes, nothing helps us express our emotions better than these words.

How about communicating clearly with us about swearing and how we all use it? How about letting us know how their use can affect others?

How about using candour to teach us when to completely avoid profanity and when we can get away with it?

Since it is going to stay, let us not conceal the truth by being uptight and obnoxiously moral.

---

[107]http://time.com/4602680/profanity-research-why-we-swear/

REASON 45

All Transmission and No Reception

> 'Can you solve this problem?'
> 'Do you want to go to college?'
> 'How can you say no?'
> 'How old are you? When did you marry?'
> 'Don't do it or you will regret.'

Though these statements are made regularly by strangers, peers and friends, they impact our psyche and behaviour the most when they are used, knowingly or unknowingly, by parents.

When you guys ask a question like *'Can you do Maths?'* it almost feels like you are telling me that I can't. The tone, along with the words, convey that I am incapable but you are still being considerate to ask. It makes me seriously doubt my potential.

When you guys ask a question like *'Do you want to work after marriage?'* it conveys that it is a choice. I would have considered 'going to college' as a default setting if you didn't frame it as a choice that you are letting me exercise.

If a boy cries, he is asked, 'How can you cry?' If a girl refuses to help at home, she is scorned at with 'How can you say no?' giving her the idea that a 'no' from her is a 'no-no'. A boy can certainly cry using a whole tissue box and a girl can shout out as many nos as she wants but you frame your statements to make us feel selfish, ill-mannered and bad about ourselves.

You ask layered questions or twin sentences to establish a connection where none exists.

'You got a car. How happy is your life?' Do you seriously think buying a car will change the happiness quotient of my life?

Shared a young professional with my mother: 'When you ask my age and then supplement it with "When did you marry?" rather than asking, "Did you marry?" (Though why ask that in the first place?) it makes me feel I am doing a cardinal sin by staying unmarried.'

Such sentences are the perfect examples of the Pygmalion Effect[108]. If your words show that you expect less from us, we will not disappoint you. We will surely perform at par with your expectation. You have power over us and we fulfil your expectations.

I am trying to figure out why you guys just don't listen to us. First, you assume, for whatever reason that you know us inside out. You, for whatever reason, go on to believe that we do not know much about ourselves. You tend to reduce us to novices in handling ourselves and you tend to give yourselves a podium position in knowing us.

You know me inside out probably for the first three months of my existence outside of your body. And that period ended long ago. I live with my mind and body each day. Give me some leeway to open up.

Second, you imagine that we are children who are innocent and immature. What would we know about anything as we are such unexperienced pieces of a jumbled-up puzzle. You treat us as 'clueless', which is just the opposite of who we are. Though it

---

[108]Pygmalion Effect says higher expectations lead to an increase in performance and vice-versa.

is you who are clueless about a lot that we know, at least allow us to share what we are going through.

Third, you are these Superman figures in your heads for us, who would save us from all our problems. Since you are always in a hurry to fix us up, you do not want to hear us out. We might be looking for empathy, not a solution. We might be good with your nod, but you are so full with your advisory that you tune us out.

When you communicate with us by sending prejudiced signals, we learn it with perfection.

A friend of mine always says, 'The result was bad', rather than saying, 'My result was bad'.

He will say, 'The bike doesn't start', rather than saying, 'I can't start the bike'.

Such a nice way of deflecting ownership and making it sound as if the result and the bike do not need a doer, i.e. you. This is how we pick up your sentence-framing style and embark on our journey towards irrationality.

Parents are like Google. Google starts guessing what I am typing as soon as I key in the first alphabet. Similarly, parents do not listen to what we intend to say because they want to finish our sentences assuming that they can read our minds.

Does Google exasperate you too when you want to key in your search words? Do you remember how it makes you feel? You do not want second-guessing. You do not want so much assistance. We feel the same way.

So, we have a twin problem here. First, you talk a lot without listening. Second, the way you frame most of it.

You speak in a patronizing and commanding way where 'top-down' communication happens and a lot stays unsaid. How about working on building an observing and listening muscle? We can sort plenty of our problems the moment you decide to drop the 'Google' hat and don the 'Zen' robe to listen. We are waiting for your mouths to shut shop and ears to flutter and open their wings.

You guys frame your statements like 'I knew it all along' or 'Don't do it, you will regret' to make us feel scared and be ready to take all the blame if something fails.

Such repetitive transmissions drill a hole in our confidence and give us a throbbing heartache. How about emitting assurance rather than doubt?

REASON 46

The 'C' and 'D' Words

Two of my schoolmates dropped out of school in the middle of the academic year. Both of them had one thing in common—divorced parents.[109] Don't get me wrong. Divorces do not encourage children to dump school. But, differences, acrimony and hostility within family impact us big time. Each fight of yours frightens us. It feels like bursting of the bubble in which we lived and expected to live forever. If we are very young when you decide to part ways, we fail to learn how to trust anyone. We regress into a shell and you guys fail to notice because you have bigger battles to fight. If we are older, we don't retreat, we become aggressive. The way you have decided to leave us, we also decide to leave you with more frustration and anger from our side. Respect and love for you vanish and an indifferent anger takes over us. There are many reasons behind a nuptial bond going kaput but the casualty is the same—US.

Partners and parents in continuous conflict are more detrimental than a divorced couple. Reasons of continuous conflict could be many, they may or may not involve us but your intense arguments and regular heated exchanges make us feel vulnerable. It feels like we are constantly in a war zone laced with landmines. We stand on a shaky ground, shivering. Your conflict-handling mechanism weakens gradually. Some of you try to hide the problems initially, but we eventually find

---

[109]https://www.businessinsider.in/30-scientific-ways-your-childhood-affects-your-success-as-an-adult/articleshow/55639766.cms

out. We live in the same home, by the way. We can also easily find out if something is wrong. Also, you guys never come to know what we go through at school or social gatherings, when your conflicts become talked about.

You guys should teach us from the very beginning that some conflict is normal and neutral. You should also keep us prepared that anything can go wrong anytime, so that we do not end up depressed and disillusioned on witnessing sudden conflict. Don't give us pure hope of having a happy family forever if your polarized personalities will get in the way.

Why couldn't you check your compatibility better before playfully getting pregnant? Why couldn't you review your commitments before putting us through your wreckage? Is there no 'family' guarantee or warranty clause that you guys need to honour? Why can't we make you pledge to give us a sane, bonded family the way you force us to be the best children?

You feel free to break our family, our nest. Not only this, you poison our minds against the life partner turned enemy. Your polarization makes our lives miserable. Does any report card or assessment sheet mention your failure as a parent?

I wish there was a cloud family network to mend our hearts broken by our own parents. The way new food delivery joints have a cloud kitchen model, the way iCloud takes care of data from every iPhone, why couldn't we get a cloud family in case of being dealt with an unfair pair of parents?

Replacing a spouse is easy, displacing a parent is not. Can you hand us over an app to download new parents? You guys cannot adapt, adjust, collaborate with your husband/wife, but you gloriously expect us to accept a stranger as a new but permanent fixture in our lives? Do you realize we are talking about a parent here, not a playlist?

You seem to believe that since you moved on, we need to do the same for all practical, day-to-day purposes. Do we resemble a GRWM—Get Ready with Me—video, which promises to change our look in a few minutes?

Why do two people marry? Though my knowledge and experience has no personal bent, I believe that marriage happens when two people want to spend their lives together, happily and naturally. They choose to become a team which will stay together not for external rewards or validation, but because they are intrinsically inclined to be with each other. A married couple is not forced to cooperate or collaborate. It does so for the joy of being and living together.[110] There is no obstinacy of personal ideation and personal opinion.

If you cannot give up your ego, if you cannot love the idiosyncrasies of your partner, if you have a deep urge to change him/her, if you hate monotony, please do not marry. If you marry because all your friends have gone down the aisle or your body clock is ticking fast, you will ruin your life and ours too.

Since it is one of those decisions which will change not only your lives but the lives of your children, please calm your wits and think it through before committing.

How about writing down a small post to yourself about '5 Reasons for Marrying XYZ' before changing your relationship

---

[110]Thoughts of noted Philosopher J. Krishnamurthy: 'A married couple does not come together to achieve a collective reward. In that case, the collaboration lasts till the collective goal is achieved and then it vanishes. They cooperate and collaborate because it is fun to be together.'

status online? How about doing some 'deep work' to check if you are marrying for the right reason and the right person?

A thorough 'quality check' should be done before choosing the partner and before deciding to become a parent.

If both 'quality checks' fail, the 'C' word will enter our lives. How about trying to resolve it without making us the referees? After all, if it is a long dispute, it simply means that both parties are wrong.

Though you cannot nullify the impact of your continuous conflict on us, how about cushioning the blow by not making it all pervasive in our 'routines'?

If the 'D' word is inevitable, please do not fight over us. You guys would never come to know whom we prefer.

How about respecting our emotions while planning to fight with all your might?

How about divorcing your spouse and not my parent so that I can get some co-parenting?

REASON 47

'Imbalance' Is the New 'Balance'

I searched the following topics on Google Trends: 'My wife/husband is depressed', 'My son/daughter is depressed', 'My mother/father is depressed'.

To each of these search topics, it stated that, 'Your search doesn't have enough data to show here'.

When I put, 'I am depressed', it showed peaking searches regularly. These trends prove that depression is a lonely journey. The family members would not know if others were suffering. They would not share if they were suffering.

More than five crore people are depressed in India. On an average, 371 people commit suicide daily in our country.[111] According to the World Health Organization (WHO), India is one of the most depressed nations in the world with a whopping 36 per cent Indians being depressed at some point of their lives. The stunning statistics of adults suffering from depression can cause depression all over again. The Associated Chambers of Commerce and Industry in India (Assocham) reports that the rate of anxiety and depression among corporate employees increased by 45 to 50 per cent between 2008 and 2015.[112]

Parents neither admit their blues to themselves nor share it with others. Most couples are unhappy doing what they do, living how they live, but are scared to break the routine. They

---

[111] https://www.huffingtonpost.in/2017/02/24/over-five-crore-indians-suffered-from-depression-in-2015-say-wh_a_21720760/
[112] http://www.assocham.org/newsdetail.php?id=4918

feel stuck but do not know how to hustle. I fail to understand why our parents are overworked and overstressed. Why have they accepted it to be the way of life? Isn't it possible to interact more and build less walls around? Isn't it possible to earn little less money and earn more happy time?

Depression among unhappy moms and tired dads primes us towards feeling sad, frustrated, lost and lonely. Children of depressed parents are themselves at a high risk of being depressed.[113]

It is a scary spiral:

depressed mom → uncontrollable toddler → more depressed mom → an angry tween → further depressed mom → an alienated and tormented teen

So many of our friends are rotating in this downward spiral, knowingly or unknowingly.

When you guys lose your emotional balance, it gets difficult to know who is the parent. We need to support and love you, push you to take care of yourself, check on your thoughts and behaviours.

Your emotional imbalance requires us to parent you. Does anyone realize how hard and nerve-racking that is?

Postnatal depression is the most common form of depression. Young and new moms fail to convey their fragile state of minds to anyone. They feel confined, restricted and tired all the time. They feel fatigued and bored, which causes low self-esteem and anxiety. Nobody takes their woes seriously as everyone considers it to be normal. How about nipping this

---

[113]https://psychcentral.com/lib/depressed-parents-and-the-effects-on-their-children/

depression in the bud? How about recognizing it and getting it treated?

Many of my friends live with their parents but do not know them because they live masked, trapped and unfulfilled lives. They reiterate that their families rock, but whom are they fooling? Each ideal family portrait stands on a dysfunction—an unaddressed pain, an unsolved puzzle hidden in the soul of the family.

Why do we pretend family solidarity when we feel solitary within? A respondent wrote:

'My mother doesn't know if I am anxious or depressed because I give my best to fake it.

'I do not know if my mother is deeply unhappy staying at home, waiting non-stop for all of us because she hides her puffy eyes. My father doesn't know what surges in my heart because I never expect him to understand. I do not know what my father is battling with because he never lowers his defences.'

You, as parents, try to retain the familiar turf and postpone confronting the uncomfortable front behind which lies the debris of unheard grudges and faceless fears.

And then, it topples suddenly one day, leaving behind shocking revelations and unending accusations. There are more fake families out there than the real ones. We do not acknowledge the elephant in the room unless it demolishes the room.

How about baring our souls to each other before it gets too late? How about handling the bull by its horns at the first grunt only?

A Walmart research shows that consumers expect a response in 10 milliseconds when they hit the buy or send or search button. Transactions are lost over a delay of half a second. All these transactions are generally being made by wise adults who constantly grumble that children today do not have any patience. The way tails disappeared from our bodies when not used for long, patience would disappear soon. 'To wait' is 'to wail'. I agree when you say that children today have no patience. Would you agree when I say that 'you started the game'? Waiting is a sin no one wants to commit. With parents losing their patience permanently, how would we be able to control our anger or temptations?

India has the highest number of obese people in the world. A huge number of them are parents who do not bother about their fitness. Obese parents increase the likelihood of obesity in their children[114] because of genetic and psychological influence.

Obese or unhealthy parents permit their children to ignore physical exercise and allow them to compromise on their eating habits. If 39 per cent of adults aged 18 and above were overweight and 13 per cent were obese in 2014, there is an imbalance in the lives of adults who complain about children turning into couch potatoes.

How are we going to be fit when you guys embarrass weighing scales without any guilt?

The spending habits of Indian adults are undergoing a sea change especially among elite and affluent classes, whose number is on the rise. Our parents spend far more on lifestyle considerations than previous generations and, hence, we are exposed to the best of education, clothing, automobiles, gadgets, travel and entertainment. These luxuries are like vitamins which give a feeling of enhancing our well-being.

---

[114]https://www.livemint.com/Leisure/bYDJTJjcH3Ddgz1uHaqkQO/Obesity-Indias-big-problem.html

As we continue to consume the luxuries, they become a habit. They become like painkillers which help us alleviate the itch of discomfort.

A luxury car or branded apparel which was a vitamin earlier becomes a painkiller. Not having a luxury car or branded apparel becomes a pain.

You guys are gifting us privileges which become 'our life support'. We get 'hooked' to comfort and luxury.

How am I expected to walk in the sun when my walks have always ended at the door of an automobile?

How am I supposed to learn to budget my expenditure if you swipe a credit card whenever I wish?

Depression, obesity and over-spending signal a lack of psychological, physical and financial balance. Aren't you gifting it to us as our legacy? How about welcoming patience in our lives? How about making tiny habits to exercise and eat healthy every day? How about talking to us about money and its importance as soon as we start voicing our demands?

REASON 48

Don't Change the Channel

You guys send me to a top-notch international school where sex education begins from Class VI. Also, how can you forget that I have been scoring pretty well in biology? Equipped with my school-imparted dry knowledge and friends-imparted gossipy gyan, I am in a pretty sorted place. Still you guys sheepishly change channels and talk loudly to me whenever we watch movies or shows together and the screen shows anything remotely romantic. Dad turns into an awkward goofball around his 16-year-old whenever a kissing scene comes on screen. He is my personal censor board who hardly ever watches any film with me apart from *The Adventures of Tintin* and *The Secret Life of Pets*. He shies away from stepping into any movie theatre with me and is usually uncomfortable if that ever happens. Though we tactfully sit as far away from each other as we can, the tremors emanating from his discomfort and embarrassment reach me easily.

If he ever reads this, I want him to know: I watch *Friends* and AIB videos WITH Mom.

All the time.

I understand Joey's sex jokes and know about Rachel's 'Dirty Book'[115].

Why do you pretend that time is standing still for you and me?

---

[115]https://www.youtube.com/watch?v=gNdfNhzGF7s

Maintaining a distance is a sign of respect for you.

Maintaining openness is a sign of deeper respect for me.

I am closer to you when I can confide my deepest questions in you. Ignoring questions about sex or love, as if they don't exist, is hypocrisy at its highest level. We exist because you guys indulged in sex. Are you ashamed of accepting it or you want us to believe that we were Godsend!

It is your attitude that distorts our thoughts about attraction, sex and relationships. Since you prefer to hide everything around sex, we all play hide and seek. It doesn't mean that we are neither experimenting nor getting worked up, it simply means that we are hiding it from you. The mask of being 'beyond sex' is one of the biggest shams of a parent–child relationship which begins with 'having sex'.

The 'social desirability bias' forces you to be socially acceptable and hence you would never talk about something that tarnishes your self-righteous image.

You, as parents, are always curious to know what are we doing on our phones and laptops. We, as children, are curious about your usage and we sneak into your devices whenever we get a chance.

What we see is shocking, to say the least. Whatever you say to us, share on your social networking handles, fill in various surveys and research reports, speak less about you than what the history of your Internet searches can reveal.[116]

I can already feel your rolling eyes on reading the term PDA (Public Display of Affection). 'Why are children these

---

[116] Seth Stephens-Davidowitz. 2017. *Everybody Lies: Big Data, New Data, And What The Internet Can Tell Us About Who We Really Are*. New York: HarperCollins.

days so hooked on PDA?' is what would honk in your head.

Wait before you whine. My PDA is *partner display of affection*—some show of affection between the husband and wife whom we call parents.

My grandparents, as you guys mention all the time, never showed any love or affection, publicly or privately, even towards their children, i.e. you. But you guys show affection (to some extent) towards me. When I was young, I received some doses of hugs, which are dwindling as I am growing up.

However, I have never seen you both getting cozy and showing any signs of being romantic companions. Presence of any physical chemistry and connection between you two seems as remote a possibility as getting Wi-Fi in my bathroom.

Believe me, I cringe openly when I see my classmates getting all over each other.

It's all your fault. You neither upload any family pictures nor get intimate in front of me or the camera. You inspired me to never have an FB account as you would have freaked out if I posted any picture of mine. This is a very personal disappointment as my friends are very comfortable with physical proximity in fiercely public spaces. I believe their parents might have shared a little partner display of affection.

My friends talk about 'making out' more often than they talk about school grades while I remain touch-repellent.

Why can't you guys be a little normal and natural? Were you like this before my birth too? Do you wish to let me grow into a person who considers physical show of affection to be inappropriate?

Why do you feel embarrassed in showing a natural emotion? Why do you find it unnecessary?

I crave for a MOMMY HUG and a DADDY KISS. I certainly wish to go beyond, but the mere thought freaks me out. Thanks to your bipolar behaviour which showers kisses on me but becomes impervious towards each other. How about allowing some intimacy to enter between you two?

REASON 49

ATMs or Dads

'Any fool can have a child. That does not make you a father. It is the courage to raise a child that makes you a father,' says Barack Obama.

I have been an admirer of Barack Obama as a parent. During the eight years of his presidency, he had been an involved father. He planned to wear sunglasses for his daughter's graduation ceremony so that he could cry!

If a president can take out time to be with his daughter, if a president can show his emotions as a father, then other fathers would need to dig really deep for reasonable excuses for being passive fathers.

A friend of my father commented that his role in the life of his children is that of an ATM. Though I didn't quite understand whether he felt great or distressed or nothing about it, I realized that fathers, or the andro part of a couple, play a dormant role. They are more of a sleeping partner in the family venture. The reasons are many:

- Men want everyone to believe that they are up for higher goals. They put in extra effort to make us believe that they are terrifyingly tied up at work. Fathers are experts at showing that they are busy. Digital media has facilitated all the dads who, while browsing the Internet, show that they are busy answering important mails and calls. Dads get the luxury of being tired and being neck deep in work, because moms are naïve

and accommodative. Dads can afford to flaunt their unavailability because moms stand behind them, like a rock, to fill in.
- Cooking and cleaning, housekeeping and caregiving didn't come installed in a woman's DNA. Apart from giving birth to a child, nothing else falls strictly in a male or female domain. A dad can cook and a mom can file a tax return. But dads have attached higher meaning to filing tax returns, which are done monthly or annually, than cooking or cleaning which is to be done at least twice a day.
- Fathers remain in the backseat because mothers do not want to give up their driver seats. They do not even like collaborations which they see as 'intrusions' or 'invasion' of their mommyland! A husband and a wife divide their turfs, admittedly, to reduce conflict. Both like to protect their own bastions. I wonder sometimes if my parents collaborate or compete. The division of labour turns Dads into ATMs and Moms into smartphones.
- Parents of adolescents feel that children have no time for them as they are busy with their own engagements. This is how we have felt throughout our childhoods. I remember my Dad playing his own creative games with me till I was 5. After that, he got bored of being a Dad every day and started enjoying only his own hobbies.
- Fathers do not have role models to emulate. Our culture commemorates distant fathers who are stoic like rocks and authoritative like kings. So, it needs courage on their part to change the diapers of their children or comb their hair or feed them. The parents of a friend

of mine are senior police officials. Though, both are equally busy and accountable for their professional commitments, I only see her mother at every PTM. The more hands-on fathers we get today, the better it would be for the families of tomorrow.

- Fathers do not get sufficient paternity leaves. Opting for flexi times is not the norm for fathers. The present-day fathers can take inspiration from Instagram father Austin McBroom[117] who seems to capture every step of his daughter's childhood by being an inseparable part of it.

Fathers, to maintain their stature, use their 'provider tag' as a double-edged sword:

'I am the provider of the family. Since I pay the bills, I deserve more respect and gratitude.'

'I am merely the provider. I am only remembered to pay the bills. Though I deserve respect as a father and gratitude as a provider, my family, especially the children, take me for granted.'

To seek sympathy, they proclaim the 'poor father' stance of being ATMs. They don't have time to be involved in our growing-up pursuits but they wish to believe that they are ignored.

Fathers suddenly get interested in our lives when we are knocking on the doors of adulthood. We are not used to these heightened bouts of interest but they want all the attention just because they are obliging us by getting interested.

Moms genuinely get bored of us but hang on in absence of

---

[117] Check Austin McBroom's Instagram account: https://www.instagram.com/austinmcbroom/?hl=en

alternatives. We also get terribly bored of mothers every day. Some involvement of fathers might do some good to all of us. It will be a change of perspective and evolution of shared ground. Some 'job rotation' at home will be beneficial for all of us. A 'Watching TV Dad' and a 'Cooking Missile Mom' can swap roles.

Moms should certainly demand weekly offs away from their families so that they are recharged and we realize their value.

I have this friend in school who prefers smiling to speaking. On a rare occasion, we were having lunch and he spoke:

'I saw your film. Cool stuff.'

'Thanks.'

He shrugged.

'Did you watch it at the school festival?'

'Ya.'

'Started working on college applications?' I couldn't think of anything else to say. The heaviest thought tumbled out.

'A little. Where do you want to go?'

After an excited one-minute monologue about my options, I asked him about his plans.

'What about you?'

He was already packing his lunch box.

'Anywhere. Don't tell anyone, but my goal is to be a real good Dad.'

He flashed his smile and left.

My film was about loving parents. Did he share his dream with me because of that? Or, did he have an itch to say it out loud to someone that day?

Whatever the reason, his words will stay. And also the smile. How about dreaming to be a Dad? How about working on this dream project? How about encouraging your sons to dream this dream?

REASON 50

Quality Time Hogwash

Time is so valuable because it never comes back. Wrong.

Time is so valuable because it keeps coming back in the form of memories frozen in the hearts.

Out of all the memories, we remember the memories of our childhoods the most. Research proves that a patient of Alzheimer's forgets everything but remembers his childhood till his last day.[118]

We remember the time spent as children because that is the carefree time without watches. We remember the time spent as children because that was the slow time where no one asked, 'What next?'

I asked many friends to recall the 'best moments of their childhood'. All of them mentioned some time spent with their families but it was never a memory from an eventful day. A friend mentioned a night when her father took her out on a scooter ride and they ran out of petrol on the way. They ended up singing all the way back home, dragging the scooter.

Another one talked about all the evenings when his father would make up a story and he would enact that absurd story.

I remember those days when my dad would ride my tricycle with me in the backseat.

I do not like quality as much as quantity when it comes to

---

[118]Daniel L. Schacter. 2001. *The Seven Sins of Memory: How the Mind Forgets and Remembers.* New York: Houghton Mifflin Company.

time with parents, because whatever my heart would remember after years will become 'quality' on its own. If I go to buy a neckpiece from a jewellery store, the salesperson surely shows me the best products. I cannot rely on his quality promise unless the product I buy stands the testament of time. I will pronounce it as a 'quality neckpiece' only after I cherish it for long. Declaration of 'quality' by the salesperson, like parents, is a post-truth.

'Quality time' is a convenient 'reframing' by parents to prove that they are present for all milestone moments that matter and their absence from mundane moments is not of much consequence. How do we explain to our parents that we need them suddenly in those fleeting moments that have no frills attached?

My best meals with my mother happen right on our kitchen platform, on nondescript nights, alongside the deepest conversations.

Once, I opened up suddenly to her while she was braiding my hair. Why don't you guys realize that we grow up on days which have no agenda.

Life happens while you are planning to design it. Your quality time begins on the dinner table where we share the happiness of the whole day, but I might be yearning to have a conversation with you as soon as I came back from school. The moment passed by the time dinner happened.

I might want to spend time every day with you guys. My 'quality time' is not congruent with your version of 'quality time'. You stress a great deal on the time spent together at different locations. These vacations come with extra exuberance and deep involvement from parents like a helping of extra cheese with the new flavour of pizza. This unnecessary involvement for a few days is annoying and far from freezing into any special memories.

God gave us gravity. No one can escape the earth's pull. Had he wanted objects to keep floating, he would have created that kind of force.

God gave us parents. No one can escape giving time to children when they are young. Had God wanted us to grow up on our own, he would have created a shorter and zero-dependence childhood.

God gave us eyelids because he needed a way to close the eyes. He did not give us ear-lids.

God gave us parents because he needed caregivers to take care of us for a long time. Had he wanted us to become self-reliant in just a few years, he would have designed you guys like birds who quickly make their babies self-reliant.

I want to 'own' your time, but your career and friends devour that time. After a few years, when you want to 'have' my time, the same story follows, in reverse.

How about getting inspired by IBM employee Lisa Seacat DeLuca who calls herself a 'motherworking' not a 'working mother'? Last year, she took her 4-month-old daughter to a conference.[119]

A friend of my mother works in Mumbai and has a lucrative job. She visits her daughter during vacations who lives with her grandparents in Rajasthan. Some friends of mine have moved to boarding schools because their parents can't make a place for them in their daily lives.

---

[119] http://www.businessinsider.in/A-famous-IBM-employee-took-her-baby-to-an-IBM-conference-and-had-to-deal-with-a-smart-aleck/articleshow/51233854.cms

Many core parts of our lifestyles are no longer our regular companions. Sari, a core part of dressing, has become a speciality product. People do not dress up traditionally every day anymore. They over-dress or dress up ostentatiously on festivals as if to compensate for not wearing kurta-pyjama or sari more often. The core part of parenting—spending time with children—is turning into a speciality to be used on special days like weekends or vacations.

I fail to understand this distorted concept of quality time. Parents define quality time as the time that THEY have conveniently for their children. 'Whatever and whenever'—at parents' disposal—becomes the exclusive, extraordinary quality time. The Halo Effect around 'quality time' is parents' justification for their absence and disinterest in our lives on a daily basis. You decide 'prime time' for our childhood channel. A strict diet for months is followed by binge eating for a few chosen days.

How about observing our emotions and listening to our needs to match them with your time on a daily basis? We can't be raised on weekends and whims.

How about letting us partner in declaring the definition of 'quality'? There is no quality certification that can confer 'quality award' on moments spent together at your convenience.

How about spending 'mindful time' with us? We can easily make out when you play with us or teach us half-heartedly, the same way you can easily make out when we study half-heartedly.

Your presence is far more important than your presents.

REASON 51

Why Did You Give Birth to Us?

Superstar Amitabh Bachchan slammed this question on his father's face one day when he was frustrated beyond measure: 'Why did you give birth to us?' Befitting his anger, the father (famous poet Harivansh Rai Bachchan) did poetic justice by answering the universal question through a poem which meant that neither my dad asked for my permission before giving birth to me, nor my grandfather asked my dad for the same, but you make a new beginning by asking for permission from your children before giving birth to them.[120]

When Mr Bachchan asked this question, he was tired of the way life was treating him.

When we ask this question during our childhood or adolescence, we are generally tired of the way our parents treat us.

'We marry primarily to have children,' said an opinion maker on national television.

'Parenting is like exercising. Once I got into it, I realized I am allergic to it,' said a fellow parent.

'Having a child is like having a government job. Nobody can take it away,' said a philosopher.

'You didn't know what it entails to be on a Ferris wheel unless you hop on it. The beginning of parenting is like getting

---

[120] https://timesofindia.indiatimes.com/life-style/relationships/soul-curry/Life-lessons-by-Harishvansh-Rai-to-an-angry-Amitabh/articleshow/46862632.cms

on a Ferris wheel. However, the similarity ends there. The Ferris ride ends but the parenting ride doesn't,' said a tired mother of four.

You decide to make babies because:

- **Everyone does it.** Would you want to live with some ever-changing devils only because others are doing so? Elders force their children to have children. After having one child, they force to have another child so that the first one does not feel lonely. (In India, they are socially coerced for a third child if the first two are girls.)
- **We are a result of extreme social pressure not passion.** We should become a doctor if we are passionate about human physiology, disease, cure, research about medicines, pain, etc. We should not become a doctor because our friend wants to become a doctor or because it is a noble and respectable profession or because a doctor character in a film inspired you or because you love how the lab coat and stethoscope feel.

    Be a carpenter if you are passionate about carpentry. Be a parent only if you are passionate about raising a child with patience, balance and discipline for a minimum of two decades. If being with kids and raising them gives you pleasure and purpose in life, have them, else let it go.
- **Some want children to complete their family.** It is a mere imagination that a family needs children. It is a mere gimmick to keep a husband and wife together, a little longer. Did you have a child to justify your marriage? Does your marriage become meaningful when you become parents? Isn't it absurd?

- **You would love to have an extension of yourself.** You like them till they are cute and behave like pets. All those people who take the pregnancy plunge to get a 'mini me' are startled to rise to the rude awakening that 'mini me' is an individual, not their obedient extension. Some couples become parents to carry on the family name, to make it immortal. How does the family name matter once you drop dead? Who knows whether the family name will shine or suffer due to your child? Some bear children for future hypothetical insurance. They believe that their children will take care of them in their twilight years.

Most of the parents who get pregnant are not ecstatic or passionate about a baby changing their lives forever. In 1975, Ann Lander conducted a survey titled, 'Do you regret having children?' and 70 per cent of respondents said 'Yes'. The enormous social pressure forces youngsters to marry and then have children. Childlessness is equalized to selfishness. Womanhood is equalized to motherhood.[121]

I doubt if all of you really wanted children. I appreciate those couples who choose not to have children over those who forgot to choose and became default parents. Their bodies gave birth but their hearts never turned into parents' heart. They remained individuals before and after the birth. Do you own your 'parenting' role or 'operate' in this role?

A girl wrote on Quora that one of her parents told her, 'If it were up to me and others were not there to question, I would have killed you by now.' She further mentioned that

---

[121] http://www.yourtango.com/my-kids-have-made-me-less-happy

some mistake of hers had angered the parent to make such a damaging comment. There are plenty of such heartbreaking comments that parents hurl at their children out of anger, out of habit, out of 'foreign' frustration, out of nothing in particular.[122]

The easiest part of parenting is to give birth to children. You guys only think till this part.

There are numerous instances which make us think, 'Why did you want us?'

Children blurt out this question when:

- **Parents have no time to spend with their children.** Parents find their professional roles very demanding and draining. Their phones keep them 'hooked' to their jobs every minute and the 'felt time' with family fades away. We are the easiest targets for parents to ignore or scream at. A job and a boss can neither be ignored or screamed at. A social engagement gives you visibility and social happiness while we are harbingers of conflict and stress.
- **Parents deem their child-rearing actions as favours done to their children.** They expect gratitude and accountability in return. Since it is made to sound like a 'give and take' transaction, it converts the parent-child connect into a personal accounting statement where the debit and credit sides must be equal.

  We should be responsible and respectful irrespective of what our parents do. If my father buys a new car

---

[122]http://www.dailymail.co.uk/femail/article-3397639/Adults-share-damaging-things-parents-said-them.html

for me, and my respect and responsibility hits a high, this would be absurd.

- **Parents get tired of the parenting role and children turn into non-performing liabilities.** Parents get mentally disengaged and emotionally detached. When the plates are too full, we suffer from many challenges. The food gets mixed and the taste gets mashed-up. Then, we need more focus to maintain the sanctity of the plate.

    The plate seems very heavy as we try to balance the eatables in their own territories on the plate. We feel tired and fail to enjoy the food.

    To keep the plate lighter and cleaner, we decide to limit the stuff on the plate. When others talk about the Italian Cuisine or the Gujarati Thali, we regret the loss.

If your plates are full, please do not add us on them because once you put us up there, you cannot get away from us easily.

If we lay unattended on the plate, we rot and the stench will suffocate all your senses.

There is an 'inherent binding' in our relationship. You can cease to be a friend, a spouse, a follower, a believer, a superior and a subordinate, but you can never cease to be a parent or a child.

The decision of being a mother or a father, a son or a daughter is 'binding'. We are like tattoos on your face. Think it through before getting them.

How about helping yourself decide by using your mind, body and soul?

How about taking time out with your spouse to figure out your family vision, mission and objectives?

I found this troubled mother on a social networking site where she shared her pain of not liking her own child because he was argumentative with everyone and made everything complex and difficult.[123]

I genuinely feel this to be a big concern where some of us are a huge perennial pain for everyone, specifically in growing-up years. You guys must be feeling cheated on being handed over a person very difficult and different from you when you had wished for a 'mini you'. It feels like ordering a camera and receiving a defective pen drive from your trusted online platform.

How about having realistic expectations from these faulty pen drives? How about realizing that the children you got are not your shadows and they come with a disclaimer—'This is an original piece. Any resemblance to any person, dead or alive, is accidental. Parents cannot be held solely responsible for how s/he turns out.'

---

[123] http://www.chabad.org/blogs/blog_cdo/aid/1264680/jewish/Not-Enjoying-Parenthood.htm

REASON 52

Have You Seen a Father Hero?

Indian culture is full of heroes whom we look up to. Mythological heroes like Lord Rama, Lord Krishna, political heroes like Gandhiji, business heroes like Rahul Bajaj, Dhirubhai Ambani or film heroes like Raj Kapoor, Rajesh Khanna, are worshipped for being rare gems. Their qualities as warriors, politicians, businessmen and actors are extolled and highlighted for lesser mortals to emulate but no one mentions their strengths as fathers.

Being a father is not heroic enough for it to garner attention. We have no heroes as fathers. Maybe, that is why the role of a father, Fatherhood, is never considered important in our culture.

Lord Rama is the epitome of human perfection. So what if he was an ignorant and absent father? Lord Krishna is the master strategist and philosopher who had several children, but there is no mention of Krishna, the father, anywhere in historical texts. There is a mention of his son Samba and his horrible actions which led to Krishna himself cursing his son. Does this mean that the most successful kingmaker and celebrated life philosopher failed as a father? Does this also mean that the failure as a father does not take away anything from the persona of an otherwise known and respected figure?

Despite being the father of the nation, Gandhiji could never be the father his children yearned for. His eldest son, Harilal, always blamed his father for controlling his life and never letting him be his own person. Failure as a father never accounted for a major drawback in Gandhiji's life.

Failing as a parent is not considered as a big failure in our ethos. No brownie points are taken away from Lord Rama or Gandhiji for not being the best dads they could have been. It actually doesn't impact their perfect personalities if they fail to fare well as parents.

Drenched in our culture, soaked in mythology, families still believe that raising children is a mother's job which doesn't require attention, especially from fathers.

Fathers suck because they do not take pride in being fathers. Our cultural roots do not celebrate fatherhood. A son would never show love or care for his son in front of his parents as a mark of respect. Loving your own son is a cause of embarrassment. This mindset makes fathers aloof and authoritative.

Most of the children who responded to my survey mentioned that the most annoying thing about their father was that he never had time for anything but to get angry. Fifty per cent of the respondents wrote that fathers would never have the patience to listen. Fathers tend to believe that they have other important matters to address than listening to a child.

Also, it is considered to be a mother's job only to raise children while fathers are busy building nations or businesses. It is believed that fathers are too busy to pay attention to less important tasks like child-rearing.

The tragedy here is:

- **Adults are not expected to be heroes as fathers.** Hence, adults who are fathers, use all their energies to be professional or social heroes. Men are not raised to nurture or show empathy. They are made to believe in rough masculinity as their default setting and, hence, they do not know how to be a caring, sharing and nurturing father. Men are appreciated for being great professionals and leaders but not for being involved fathers. That is why men do not mind ignoring their fatherhood for other feats.

It surprises everyone if a father attends school meetings, plays with his children, drops them to various classes or cooks with them in the kitchen. Those who do, are heroes in the eyes of their children.

- **Adults do not strive enough to be heroes as fathers.** It is a personal choice which requires effort—a lot of it. Only those fathers would be ready to invest in their fatherhood who are mindful of the impact that it would have on their son or daughter.

  Women have an intrinsic will and an extrinsic expectation to excel as mothers. It is just the opposite for fathers. There is insignificant extrinsic expectation to be a daily dad. An intrinsic will, too, is optional.

My dad moved to Mumbai due to his professional commitments, while I stayed back in my hometown for a few years. I was eight and had just started Class III. One day, my dad came straight from the airport to my school to pick me up. He wanted to surprise me. He told the assistant at the information desk that I study in Class I. The teacher of Class I knew me (I was the only girl named Swaraa) and she shouted at the caller for disturbing the wrong class.

When I came out, he genuinely surprised me, 'When did you come in Class III?'

This is not my story alone. I know this for sure because my father has narrated this story many a times to show his knack for being absent-minded. Whenever it is narrated, there are at least two more dads who gleefully join him and echo the same scenario. It is not a matter of embarrassment or shame, but one that generates laughter or mild surprise.

I know many of you will have an opposite story to tell about involved fathers. I say, 'More power to them. May their tribe increases!'

Our history and our culture are replete with fathers who maintained a dry distance from their children. Their sole concern was to play the role of the breadwinner and provider. The tradition continues, as the sons of today learn from their fathers. Research at University of Pennsylvania suggests that children who feel closeness and warmth with their fathers are twice as likely to enter college and half as likely to show various signs of depression.[124]

Each child wants to spend more time with his dad. Getting undivided attention from one's dad is a big life goal for every child. A father who communicates clearly and lovingly is the dream of every child.

According to the US Bureau of Census, there were 1.8 million lone fathers raising children and 1,54,000 stay-at-home dads.[125] The number is on a rise in India too. These fathers are primary parents who value their parenting role.

---

[124] https://www.focusonthefamily.com/family-q-and-a/parenting/the-significance-of-a-fathers-influence

[125] Jyotsna Pattnaik (Ed.). 2013. *Father Involvement in Young Children's Lives: A Global Analysis*. Berlin: Springer Science & Business Media. pp. 1–9.

A father can actually play the most striking role in teaching his son 'How to be the authentic man', who understands and expresses his emotional, mental and physical needs responsibly.

A father, loving and caring, would teach his son to be loving and caring.

A father, respectful and faithful, would teach his son to be respectful and faithful.

Such sons would neither tease a girl, nor throw acid on her.

If every father makes fathering a daily deed, our families will become more safe, sane and serene.

How about praising the father hero hidden in men? How about making 'competence as a father' to be one of the parameters in ascertaining the hero index of an individual?

How about taking some sheen away from a star when he fails as a father?

How about giving the 'father' in a man his due?

REASON 53

Extreme Is the New Normal

> Parenting is a trophy for you to win.
> Parenting is a style statement for you to show with swag.
> Parenting is an umbrella for you to keep open at all times.
> Parenting is a cool drink for you to enjoy.
> Parenting is a war zone for you to tolerate.
> Parenting just happened to you.

This is my version of parenting styles formed by my mother in her previous book.[126] You guys become annoying if you generally follow any of these six styles. You can become an 'AHA Parent' if you follow the ideal parenting style of Moon Parenting. That is like climbing Mount Everest every month.

I am not looking for an 'ideal place for parents and children to coexist'. I intend to create a 'work-in-progress, open place for parents and children to be happy, healthy and hopeful.'

For that, we as a family need to 'stay in the centre', ruling out an extreme right or extreme left position. We are turning into a human race that is robotically normalizing extreme behaviours. Extremes are the new normal. That is why parents, like others, are googling up more.

'A little excess' of everything—positive and negative' is setting us up for failure.

A 'Super Parent' desires 'a little more' of achievement from us. When we do not garner laurels to their benchmarked levels,

---
[126]Swati Lodha, *Don't Raise Your Children*, pp. 107–37.

they get angry and all hell breaks loose. If we become super achievers, our lives become rat races.

A 'Designer Parent' desires 'a little more' of exclusivity from us. When we are happy being regular, brand-unconscious, they feel very ordinary and left out.

If we become designer kids, our lives become 'fashion shows'.

A 'Bulletproof Parent' desires 'a little more' of protection for us. When we defy their control, they get emotional or aggressive. If we become submissive children, our lives become 'zoo cages'.

A 'YES Parent' desires 'a little more' of coolness and friendship. We are always ready for it but it makes our lives a 'spoilt party'.

A 'Polarized Parent' desires 'a little more' of support and validation from us. We can agree with either one of them and the other gets hurt. Our life resembles a 'boxing ring'.

'Island Parents' desire 'a little more' of aloofness from us. There is nothing more to lose here as everything is lost.

If parents in any of these avatars decide to dilute their desires, we will be in for a better life.

On one extreme are super parents, designer parents and bulletproof parents who expect more, spend more and protect more.

On another extreme are yes parents, polarized parents and island parents who allow more, fight more and ignore more.

How about shifting to the middle ground?

Though I am a teenager in the twenty-first century, I have been prepared for life by my very progressive grandmom.

She loves to cook on wood, and uses a small mud oven and a charcoal stove to cook amazing food.

It takes longer. It needs attention. It generates heat.

But it has a heavenly flavour, is natural and cooks to the core. It has always been a fun experience to watch and help her do this slow-cooking passionately.

While remembering those times of roasting vegetables and poppadums and cooking curries and biryanis, I figured this analogy out.

If you guys could oscillate between being 'cook on wood' parents and 'microwave oven' parents, it would be delicious.

Though it will need more time, more attention and more intensity, just imagine the unique flavours and authentic taste of your children's personality.

I know I sound like an old aunt championing old-school cooking, but I am so proud of these slow-cooking ways that have given my taste buds the best experiences.

How about changing your hurried and harried mindset into a slowly baked one?

REASON 54

*Conditions Apply

Imagine these situations:
A boy wants to smoke a cigarette. He goes to his father.

Situation 1
'Dad, I want to smoke!'
'What?' (The communication loop closes.)

Situation 2
'Dad, I want to smoke!'
'Why?' (The boy should clearly state the reason.)
'I just want to try it. My friend seemed to enjoy it. Sanjay Dutt looks real macho when he smokes.'
'This is ridiculous. Have you gone crazy?' (Communication closes, but the desire doesn't.)

Situation 3
'Dad, I want to smoke!'
'Why?'
'I just want to try it. My friend seemed to enjoy it. Sanjay Dutt looks real macho when he smokes.'
'OK! So, how and when do you want to do it?'

Any of these situations would have been possible only if the dad had been a listener to his child's earlier rants and rationales. When the father shows surprise (Situation 1) or anger (Situation 2), any opportunity for an honest and intimate communication dies. When the father becomes 'a partner in desire fulfilment' (Situation 3), he wins 'intimacy' as well as 'a foot in the door' to dilute the desire or keep it in check.

If you either do not listen or judge the desire, the honesty streak ends, the initiation of intimacy dies a premature death and I am left alone. I say this from my own experience. There is an 'insane intimacy' between my mother and me. Though I hate to admit it, she is the wall on which my mental racket throws all the tantrum balls. She is the sponge that absorbs all that I spit out. I, unabashedly and irreverently, share my thoughts, actions, plans and dreams with her. With years of arguments and sob sessions, we have trained ourselves to be this intimate, inseparable team.

Please hear me out as I consolidate my case of how creating the most intimate team with your mom/dad is the best life choice.

This team ought to be the most intimate because of:

- **Familiarity**. A mom is the most familiar with her newborn. The familiarity can remain intact by patiently and openly working on it. Nudging constantly towards 'We are a family and family comes first' will keep the close attachment. Though it needs physical presence and emotional involvement from you guys.
- **Companionship.** The mom/dad could be the best accomplice of their children if they learn to mask their facial fineries and verbal eruptions. Feel and think like a mature, rational adult but act like your child's age. It will make your camaraderie stronger than Ambuja

cement. Though it needs refined 'mirroring act' by you guys.
- **Warmth.** This relationship has an unexplainable cozy warmth which needs to be fiercely guarded against the attacks of technology, peers and environment. If the 'way back home' is always simple, visible and full of love, why would we not want to come back after every triumph or defeat? Though it needs loads of patience and unconditional love supply from you guys.
- **Understanding.** Parents can surely understand their children during all stages of childhood if they are ready to observe (without judgement) and strategically communicate (without anger) with us.

How about opening up with integrity and intimacy? The concept of 'dignified distance' between parents and children has been causing this 'generation gap' for centuries. You are ready to grumble about this gap and accept it rather than trying to gift 'intimacy with integrity' to us.

The dignity disguised as distance makes me search for friends who are as clueless as I am, websites which readily give me more than I want, strangers who are on the lookout for clueless and curious dumb heads like me.

What you could easily do by keeping all the communication channels open is barely done by all external, inadequate support that I garner for myself.

You guys annoy me when you all try to trick your children into believing that you are open and honest with them with a small footnote saying 'conditions apply'.

Earlier, any wish of yours would meet a 'No' from your parents. For us, our wishes meet a 'Ya' followed by a 'but'. The

'Ya, but' paradox that parents try, gives this impression that they started with a 'Ya' which is the more significant aspect of the decision-making process. The 'but' is mentioned only to give a clearer picture, which is actually a 'veiled no'.

As parents, you make a superficial change and try to pass it off as a signature change in the fabric of our family. Should the freedom that is 'given', be really called 'freedom'? When you give it to me, you show your generosity of handing over the freedom.

Don't show off that you are progressive and your children are free to choose certain things like their drink or the colour of the wall in their room. 'Buy a car of any colour as long as it is black', is the credo here.

When you say that you want us to be honest and open with you, it requires a signature change—a cultural shift in our family ethos. It is not like putting a 'coffee vending machine' or 'pool table' in an authoritative organization.

It is like accepting my honesty in choosing the colour of the dress that I wish to wear for my prom, but not honour the honesty principle when I talk about your behaviour. You want 'technical honesty' not 'adaptive honesty'.

Honesty means I can go and empty all my thoughts, desires, fantasies and fears in front of my parents.

Integrity means my parents can share their failures, adventures and misadventures with me, age appropriately of course.

My mother knows that she is my closest companion. I am painfully honest with her and she is brutally so. We get hurt but we have the underlying familiarity, companionship, warmth and understanding intact.

After all,

Who else would know I sneeze whenever I enter a lift and need a tissue?

Who could differentiate between a mail written by me or my classmate?

Who else would jump on the bed with me at midnight or sob with me in a theatre.

Who else would press my feet (and kiss them) when I am tired (I am not saying 'every day')?

Who else would nod furiously while I make the most biting remark about a cousin?

Who else would gradually change my mind about the same cousin?

This is my experience and it is a beautiful one. Most of the parents fail to create intimacy because their culture and their childhood experiences condition them to demand dignified distance.

They do not want to show their vulnerability to their children and, hence, we all suffer in silence or share stuff with distant people.

An intimate and vulnerable connect with our parents keeps us safe and happy.

How about creating an eternal place of safe happiness? Believe me, I think like a child and it works.

Acknowledgements

Thank God for parents.

And thank God more for theirs.

Besides God, we would also like to express our immense gratitude to all the people for being the constant support we needed:

—All the parents and children who helped us by sharing their stories through a questionnaire and a conversation.

—Rudra Narayan Sharma, Commissioning Editor at Rupa Publications, for being supportive since the beginning, and accepting our ideas with incredible understanding. To Prerna, for her meticulous edit.

—Mamta, for all the typos and laughs during the assistance provided whilst we put this book together.

—Our parents (and grandparents), for being the subjects and inspirations for this fifty-four-reason long rant.

—Shailesh, the Husband and the Dad, for giving us newer and juicier reasons each day.

www.ingramcontent.com/pod-product-compliance
Lightning Source LLC
Chambersburg PA
CBHW022053160426
43198CB00008B/221